Worldly

By

Jason Townsend

www.Facebook.com/WorldlyBook

"Oh never will the deep-throated sound of those bells quit my ear…" – Friedrich W. Nietzsche

FOREWORD

The book you are about to read is an autobiographical story and as so it is nearly entirely true. However, names have been changed to protect the anonymity of the people involved. In some instances, a character has been built to represent multiple people and in some cases events may be slightly altered for effect. Overall the story, and more importantly the point of the story, is verifiably true.

A Word About the Cover

To answer criticism directly, it was not a mistake. Jehovah's Witnesses do not believe Jesus died on a cross. They believe he died on a "torture stake". I decided to use a cross on the cover as it is a more recognizable image (the picture would look pretty confusing with a guy just carrying a log). Also, for the statement that it doesn't matter. Cross, torture stake, same thing... it seems a petty and insignificant argument over the shape of the device that The Savior died on.

WORLDLY

CHAPTER ONE

<u>Lancaster, PA</u>

It was a gray Monday morning. The sun was behind a thick cloud layer and the clouds were behind the trees. So many trees. A sunrise is rarely noticed on a day like this, too much is happening to care, but I remember now. It was cold… damn cold. The evergreens were dusted in white, and beside my road ran a busy little creek (say *crick)* that miles later emptied into the Susquehanna River. A snow plow had come down, maybe hours before, and pushed freshly-lain snow to the banks of River Road. A salt truck had followed it, melting the remainder as a gray, wet slush. Other than that, it looked beautiful- like a model missing a front tooth.

A big yellow school bus came barreling down our narrow country road. On that bus my schoolmates were raising hell. Little hands slapped at the vinyl bench seats as they gloated

Townsend

about their Christmas winnings. A girl showed off her new Polly Pocket, as the boys tried to top each other's stories; it had been a white Christmas. In rowdy excitement, too early for most adults, the kids threw a Hacky Sack back and forth. The children screamed in excitement as the bus driver listened to a small AM radio show about the Philadelphia Eagles. He swallowed his irritation, trying his best to ignore the children and navigate the slick road.

I watched my mother from the back seat of our 1985 Honda Accord and my mother watched the bus. We sat at the end of our driveway, on the edge of our two acres of woods called "The Sycamores". I turned my gaze to the yellow bus and wondered if it was going too fast in the snow. I nervously rubbed my pant legs and wrung my hands. A sharp tightness in my chest sped up my breathing. This prompted my mother's attention through the rear-view mirror.

"Are you nervous, Baby?"

I stopped rubbing my pant legs and turned my blank gaze out of the car window. I was mortified of both that school bus, and the place it was going.

WORLDLY

"No Momma, I'm OK." I responded sheepishly.

My mother did not believe that fraudulence, not one bit. My mom had known me for a total of six whole years and already knew me better than she knew herself. She gave a worried look that permeated through the rearview mirror before she got out of the car and opened the back door. She leaned in and scratched my back for an entire minute until I calmed down. I did not know it then, but I would never meet another human being who cared about me as much as she did then, but it would not last.

"Right... well just say a little prayer to Jehovah. You will be OK." She sighed and said, partially to herself.

My mother got back in the driver's seat, cleared her throat and adjusted her large, blocky, eighties-era glasses. She had just gotten a perm and her locks were as tight as my clenched fists. I took comfort in her new Yves Saint Laurent perfume, Opium. I had loved that smell. It reminded me of her every time I caught a whiff, and I would give an offended look to any other woman who dared smelled like her. The bottle was a gift from a man, a man whose house she cleaned- my mother would never buy something that trendy. She would also never in a million years buy a perfume named "Opium". My father had put a piece of duct tape over the name but eventually her conscience would finally outweigh her fondness of the product. She would end up throwing the bottle in the trash and switch back to an old perfume from Avon that had started to smell like alcohol. I think my parents respected the Avon business model.

The school bus drove past our driveway and kicked slush onto the front of our gray Honda. My mother looked back at us one more time, this time checking on my baby sister, Louise. Louise sat looking out the window from her car seat. Concern struck Mom, a deep inner suffering for her two obedient children. As always though, my mother wasted but a moment on such a thought, and so she put her head down and pressed on. Our 1985 Honda Accord left the snow-blanketed Sycamores and followed the school bus down River Road through a dirty aggregate of salted snow. The ride to elementary school was not too bad on a sunny day when the roads were clear, roughly a twenty-minute ride. On a day like today however, it took forty-five minutes. My mother carefully followed the school bus, never passing it... better safe than sorry. Every time it stopped, classmates would peer out of the bus and try to see who was in our car. Every time, I hid my face. Instead I tried to focus on the scenery of the ride.

Conestoga, Pennsylvania, is beautiful any day of the year, but even more so on that kind of day. I looked out at the modest homes sparsely scattered along the road. Many of them belching smoke from wood-burning stoves; I could smell it... even in the car. Firewood stacked neatly on the porch next to a rocking chair, some houses were downright country-cozy. Other houses were country-trashed, cluttered by a diverse graveyard of dead vehicles in the front yard, their guts scattered about. Funny, it was always the latter that would have a confederate flag hanging from the porch. Never the nice houses, the ones I liked to look at. Whenever we saw a confederate flag my mother would smirk and glare at it as we drove by, so I would do the same, trying to light it on fire with my mind. Pennsylvania was the North, considerably. Lancaster, Pennsylvania, was even the capital of the United States for a single day. Why the hell anyone would fly the flag of The Confederate States of America in Pennsylvania is beyond me, it just seemed like a treasonous identity crisis.

I looked out the window as our car passed an Amish farm. I watched as children ran about helping the parents work the morning chores. I was kind of jealous. They looked happy, as if they were really free. We passed a bar called Frogtown Café. To think of it now, I think of three bikers getting into a brawl on the front porch. It seems to me to be the kind of place where the Hell's Angels would keep a room to have their chapter meetings, there were always more motorcycles than cars in the parking lot. However, on that day as a six-year-old boy, I looked at the bar and only saw the mural on the outside of the building. It was a giant painting of a carefree cartoon frog wearing a crown, painted in bold colors. I loved it and wondered if they served french fries and gravy. I would never find out what it was like inside Frogtown Café. I would never make it inside.

I was in the middle of my daydream when it was abruptly interrupted by the front tire of our Honda skidding in to the curb of the elementary school. Several children (now exiting the school bus) turned to point and laugh, sending little puffs of fog in to the frigid air. Just like that, my nice car ride was over, and D-Day had come. My mother escorted my sister and me to my first-grade classroom.

The scratchy sound of the principal's voice echoed in the hallways as she made her morning announcements over the loudspeakers in each room. The echo reminded me of the sheer size of this place, I mean, God... intimidating-especially to a six-year-old. The principal welcomed us back from Christmas vacation. Out of the corner of my eye I watched my mother who stood in the front corner of my first-grade classroom. My sister sucked on a pacifier in her car seat, now perched on the teacher's desk. The announcements came to an end and my teacher, Ms. Gutshall, took over.

"OK. Class. Listen up, in case anyone forgot: every morning after announcements we will turn to the flag of The United States of America, put our hand over our hearts and recite The Pledge," Ms. Gutshall bellowed.

I shot a panicked look at my mother who sternly shook her head, *no.* My palms were so sweaty that if I did put my hand on my chest I would probably have soaked a palm print into my shirt.

"OK, hand over your hearts, like this. Remember how it goes..." my teacher continued.

A little confused, I began to raise my hand. I glanced back at my mother who looked like I was about to defecate on the floor, right there in front of everyone. She was now violently shaking her head and swatting her hand at me. I swiftly dropped my right hand to my side. The class did a pretty lousy job of saluting the flag. I guess it's a little tough to retain at age six. I stood there motionless and silent as the rest of my peers struggled through the salute. I kind of felt as if I was doing something bad, even though my mother had told me otherwise. All I knew was I just wanted to go home and watch Willy Wonka and the Chocolate Factory with her. I looked in Ms. Gutshall's direction; she gave me a reassuring nod, so I calmed down, briefly.

"OK class. Take your seats now. Everyone sit!" she hollered.

A few of the other children continued giggling, testing Gutshall's patience.

"*SIT!*" Ms. Gutshall shouted almost frantically. This brought the class to a dead halt, all eyes center stage.

Her tone immediately snapped from a psychotic shriek to a warm sunny breeze of tranquility. A first-grade teacher must have better command over the emotions they show than a jockey has over his horse.

She continued in her tranquil voice, "OK, class, we have a visitor this morning! This is Missus Miller, Jason's mom. She'd like to tell us a few things to help us get to know Jason and maybe answer any questions we might have!"

Missus, I rarely heard my mother addressed that way... it sounded weird. To me, my mother was Sister Miller. My mom smiled at my teacher and moved front and center to address my class. She wrote her name on the blackboard. My teacher buried her forehead in her hand. This was going to suck, and Ms. Gutshall was beginning to see it coming.

"OK! Class!"

"Good morning everybody! My name is Mary Miller and I am here to explain a few things to you about my son, Jason. I understand some of you have noticed some differences. You see, Jason... stand up Jason, come on." My mother said while she roasted me over an open nuclear fire.

I stood there as stiff as a ninth-grader's sock.

Townsend

She continued, "You may notice throughout the school year that Jason will participate in some things a little differently than you will. As part of Jason's belief in God he will not be part of any birthday or holiday celebrations. This does not mean that he does not like you, or that we're not all excited that you're turning seven…"

My mom chuckled alone and when she realized it, cleared her throat.

"It…a…just means that Jason and his family do not have birthday parties." You see, in the Bible, King Herod…"

My teacher cleared her throat, interrupting my mom. My mother reevaluated her approach.

"Well. Jason won't be celebrating any holidays. While you were on break, he didn't celebrate Christmas…" Mom continued.

"*WHAT?*" A wily little girl named Jenny interrupted as if she had just been electrocuted by my mother's words. A look of sheer horror was plastered on her face. Shortly after,

WORLDLY

Jenny's friend Angie was also asking why Santa did not visit my house.

"There is no…" I began but was immediately interrupted by my mother raising her voice over mine. She turned to address Angie.

"*No dear…* we do not celebrate Christmas. Santa isn't allowed on our property." She chuckled to herself.

That statement confused the hell out of me. I thought there was no Santa, period. Here my infallible mother was telling my peer he just "isn't allowed on the property". At this point my mind was racing with questions, and I was apt to pull my mother aside for questioning. Fortunately for her, she caught the look on my face and backtracked.

"OK, OK! No Easter. No Fourth of July. *Definitely* no Halloween. As Christians we know the roots of these holidays all tie to something we do not *want* to celebrate," she said, gaining back control of the room.

Angie, a polite and neatly dressed little girl sporting a gold-cross necklace started to show a very confused look. She scowled in my mother's direction as if she were Adolf Hitler.

Townsend

"It's something we do not agree with. So, Jason will not be participating in birthday and holiday activities and please don't ask him how his Christmas was. If anyone has any questions, I'll leave some… reading material… *here,"* my mom said as she reached into her large purse and ungracefully slapped a stack of Bible tracts on the corner of the teacher's desk.

The teacher was trying to not look horrified and was doing a shit job of it. Ms. Gutshall went to stop my mom but gave in and let her do it anyway. My mom fetched my sister from Ms. Gutshall's desk, smiled and left the room. My heart began to sink but just as it did my mother reappeared, poking her head back into the room.

"Your parents, you can give one to your *parents.* In case, you know, they have questions. *FEEL FREE!* The tracts. They're free!" My mom solicited, nodding to the stack of tracts on the teacher's desk.

I stared at that stack, it seemed to glow. I could make out the religious artwork on the cover. It was something so familiar to me. I had studied them, handed them out with my parents, and made paper airplanes out of them. It seemed odd to me the way they looked sitting in this environment, in public school, on my teacher's desk. Mom again resumed her trot towards the exit.

"Where were you in kindergarten?" the boy sat next to me asked. I felt the blood rush to my face.

"He didn't go to kindergarten, dear!" my mom shouted, answering in my place.

"*He was home learning to read...*" I heard her mutter under her breath as she left the room.

My mother was temporarily gone, politely ushered out of the classroom by the teacher. However, for the third time she poked her head back in the classroom. She forgot to blow me a kiss. I wonder just how loud my forehead smacking the desk sounded. She came in, made a spectacle of me, and threw me to the wolves. Now I was alone in the dark and surrounded by seething wolf cubs.

Jenny smiled at me. I don't know if it was out of pity or interest, but it appeared genuine. They say children are unforgiving, but at the same time they can be exceptionally the opposite. Jenny's friend definitely was not the exception.

Townsend

Angie's cross necklace swung like a pendulum from her neck as she stomped up to the teacher's desk. Ms. Gutshall watched her with mild trepidation but decided to let her be. Angie glared up at her as she snatched a tract from the pile. She carried the thing like a dead fish (I could almost feel her glare, though my forehead remained cemented to my desktop) as she stomped back to her desk. Once there, she carefully unzipped her backpack with one hand and dropped it in.

***

My seven-year-old butt was cold. If you've ever sat in a school hallway I'm sure you have felt it. The floor waxed to a shine that belonged on a Corvette, you could eat off it. Maybe you were a bad kid, one of those disruptive types that would be sent to the hallway when you got too excited, but that wasn't my case.

I sat on the cold polished floor with my back against the painted block wall. As I sat there I kind of enjoyed the solitude. It was a brief break. My teacher interrupted the silence as she presented me a large ziplock bag. I recognized the bag because I had helped to fill it. I remember my mother and I filled that plastic bag with Snickers, Cow Tails, Necco Wafers and packs of gummy snacks. My delicate and kind second grade teacher, Mrs. Andrews, smiled at me as if I were pathetic. She clearly felt sorry for me; I was completely oblivious as to why.

She stood over me and bent at the knees. Suddenly she and the bag were eye level. My mouth watered. I looked into her forlorn eyes and gave her my biggest grin as I picked out a solitary pack of fruit snacks. I was saving the Cow Tails and the Necco Wafers for later in the year. There would be plenty more occasions. *Through faith and patience inherit the promises-* as the good book says. Mrs. Andrews returned to her feet and zipped the bag closed. I stared at my bag of fruit snacks, I wanted to take my time and really savor it. I guess I looked pathetic because Mrs. Andrews, ever so slightly, started to cry. Her sympathetic eyes welled up with tears and she quickly turned away, returning to the classroom. When she opened the door, I could hear my classmates singing Happy Birthday. The heavy wooden door closed, and the hallway again returned to silence. I was in the hall alone with the fruit snacks.

You see, back then holidays and birthdays were openly celebrated in Pennsylvania classrooms. So, every time, I sat in the hallway by myself eating a snack from my special bag of treats and feeling sorry for the other children. The truth is, I never had much time to feel left out when I was young, and really, I wasn't left out at all.

Our day was not over when the family got home from school and work. We often got home in a rush to get ready for the next thing. I spent so much time in that building called a Kingdom Hall. A Kingdom Hall is just the Jehovah's Witnesses' word for a church. Commercial glue-down carpet. Bright fluorescent lighting up in the ceiling tiles. Upholstered stadium seating instead of pews. Grand-looking faux plants in the corners. A two-step stage with a podium front and center, a table and two chairs to the side. *No windows*. Once we attended a Hall that actually had windows and one Sunday morning a beer bottle came crashing through it.

The truth is, I never had much time to feel left out when I was a kid, although most normal kids would say I was severely excluded from even the most basic childhood pleasures. Those things aside, I was part of something, something exclusive (cults tend to be that way). I thought this life was huge and of greater importance than secular education. It was the only way to live. At least three days a week I spent a couple hours at meetings in the Kingdom Hall with my family. At bare minimum we went out preaching on Saturdays, meeting at someone's house in the morning to arrange our carpool groups. The days in between were spent studying as a family for the upcoming meetings. Every few months or so since the age of about nine, I'd be given an assignment to study and present as a talk to the congregation. I would stand at the podium in front of a congregation of roughly one-hundred, read a passage from the Scriptures and deliver an analysis of that passage. Of course, my reference material always came from the meticulously crafted books courtesy of the Watchtower Bible and Tract Association, not an outside source of reference. To be fair, there was no such thing as Google yet. Hell, the Internet was barely even something everyday people used.

It was Saturday mornings that left a lasting impression on me. With a soldier's sense of duty, we fulfilled our marching orders delivered by the Bible in Matthew 24:14- *and*

Townsend

this good news of the kingdom will be preached in all the inhabited earth for a witness to all the nations, and then the end will come. To the deepest depths of my young soul I felt a compelling responsibility to the 'worldly', to save them from missing out and being damned to eternal death. As a young child I looked out to the world with loving and curious eyes but saw only what I was taught to see. I saw people, people far too like me to abandon, but people that had the potential to destroy me. I felt as if I would not be truly happy until every single human being had seen the error of their ways and joined me under the roof of Kingdom Hall. I sure tried. From the time my little hand could reach a doorbell I was out ringing them, doing my duty to God (and man) with a solid iron conscious. Trying to save *you,* the funny thing is... no one was ever particularly grateful. They call it a few things: witnessing, ministry, service, going door-to-door, and preaching.

I remember the ministry one January morning in a trailer park standing in front of a certain mobile home. I was nine years old. A light blanket of snow had tried its best to cover up the man's mess. Tarps covered gaping holes in the roof of the trailer. Motorcycle parts littered the lot. A greasy mechanics shirt, hosting a patch embroidered with the name "Chet," lay draped over a hodgepodge Harley. An old Ford pickup truck sat in the gravel driveway. It looked as if it had been through years of war with the elements and finally surrendered. I scratched my head wondering which one of Chet's two prized pieces of shit took him on his beer runs. It occurred to me there could be a third. Maybe Chet, at that very moment, was out on his riding lawnmower buying his morning beer. I desperately hoped so. I wanted to save everyone, but some houses just gave me the creeps. I would rather leave the life-saving at places like this to someone more like my father.

Uneasy feeling aside, there I stood with my mother, dressed to the hilt. I wore a tie and a dress coat, my mother in a long skirt, blouse and warm overcoat. I imagine it looked a bit like oil in water as we stood in the front yard of this trailer that lacked at least half of its underpinning. I wondered what lived under there. There was a four-step metal stoop that led to the front door of this trailer, and boy, was it dangerously steep. Standing on the second step, my mother's head only reached about halfway up the door. Any closer and if Chet answered, my mother might fall right into the trailer. My head barely reached the bottom of the door as I sat perched on the

Townsend

first step, ready to make a run for it. I've been chased by mangy dogs before and I have learned to think ahead. I wondered what my mother was thinking as she stared intently, with a sharp seriousness at the vinyl front door. She cleared her throat, straightened her skirt and pulled her long coat closed. John Fogerty nearly knocked us straight off the stoop. Two things had just become apparent, Chet was indeed home and we had impeccable timing. A Creedence Clearwater Revival song blasted through the cold, quiet morning air.

"Never mind that music, Jason." My mother turned to me and said, still wearing her serious face.

My mother delivered three, hard knocks to the door. A Witness will learn young there are several kinds of knocks in your toolbox. There is a soft knock delivered by the middle phalanx or the flat front of the four fingers in a fist. You use this knock if you know the person is home, awake, and right on the other side of that door. It is in your best interest not to startle the homeowner, as that will lower your chances-considering they will already be pissed off once they answer the door. If that knock doesn't work, then dig into your ministry toolbox and upgrade to the Knuckle Knock. The Knuckle Knock is delivered by the proximal interphalangeal joint, the second joint down from the tip of the finger. Using the dominate index finger, bounce that first knuckle off the door surface and it will yield that satisfying "knock, knock" we have all come to despise. Add additional fingers as necessary to intensify.

My mother delivered a full four-finger Knuckle Knock. I feared it was a bit much, but my mother doesn't fuck around, and she was not going to let CCR come between her and the potential of a saved human life. By the looks of it, Chet needed saving, and *something* was definitely after him. Chet, at the very least, had a bitchin' stereo, and the low rumble of the music suddenly turned to a deafening blast as the door swung open. We leaned back about ten degrees as the music (and the sight of Chet) hit us.

"*What?* What do you want?" Chet greeted.

He peered down at us from a now open doorway, buck naked. My mother turned her head slightly as the unfortunate angle of the stoop left her face to *uh*, head... with Little Chet. I cringed and turned away at the sight of Chet's beer bludgeoned body and uncircumcised genitalia- noticing he had already started his Keystone breakfast. We were not able

Townsend

to save Chet from damnation that day, but I think he got a kick out of the encounter.

I remember the sound of horse shoes clacking on the pavement of Lancaster County roads, those black buggies with an orange reflective triangle in horse's tow. Freshly paved roads stood no chance in Amish Country. Before long they would be torn to bits by horse shoes, steel wheels and salt trucks. Softer, rubber inflated tires are frivolous to the Amish, and Road Apples, as we called them, lined the middle of each lane- horse shit.

I wondered why they chose such an appetizing name for horse shit as once again my mother and I stood on another porch. This time it was an Amish porch. Gaining no answer from a solid Knuckle Knock, my mother turned to scan the fields. She located an Amish man driving a horse drawn cart of feed into his dairy barn. My mother darted after the long-bearded man and I plunked right into a 'Road Apple'. My mom was a kind of secret agent for the preaching in Lancaster as her Swiss father had taught her German.

"Hello!" My mother greeted.

WORLDLY

The Amish man looked uninterested as could be, refusing to even turn his head to acknowledge us.

"Kein Englisch" The Amish man responded- or "*No English*".

"Verstehen Sie Deutsch?" My mother responded- or "*Do you understand German?*".

The Amish man sighed and reined in his horses. He handed the reins to a couple of interested children. They had appeared from somewhere and were curiously staring at us. Now we had his attention.

"What do you want?" the frustrated man asked, in perfect English.

Perhaps we could have tempted him with electricity, telephones or cars with fancy chrome bumpers and all. Nothing we said or tried ever worked. Not once did I see an Amish person leave their faith for ours. It was the effort that counted, but I would lose sleep over the idea of their eternal death. I would pray something would happen to make them all see the light and miraculously join our faith. We could really use some good farmers in The New World; after all, the planet would be starting over with a clean slate.

From time to time something embarrassing enough would happen to get under my skin. My mother and I stood again on the porch of an unfamiliar house. This time it was what I believed was a nicer home, in a housing development. I folded my little mittens over my pea coat and shuddered. My mom put a hand behind my neck and the shuddering stopped immediately. I gave her the smile she loved in return. She grinned back at me and I returned my hands to my side, giving the proper stance of a soldier of Jesus. I wondered if God had a way of doing this to calm earthly Jesus down when he got nervous.

Once again, my mother delivered a knock to the front door, this time a softer middle-phalanx-knock, due to noticeable noise in the house. In no time at all the door swung open and there stood Jenny from class. She smiled at me, the ten-year-old blood drained from my face, and my heart dropped into my bowels. I suddenly felt the urge to shit. To make matters worse her chubby and obnoxious brother approached from behind. He returned his spoon to his cereal bowl and used his free hand to point while he laughed at me. He pushed past Jenny, annoying her too.

"Move, Jenny, shit. What d'ya want, *JASON?* Little fag! Cool tie... *psych!*" Dave mocked as I stared and imagined an axe into his forehead.

Dave leaned in and flicked my favorite Mickey Mouse tie. Yeah, I was probably a little old for such a tie, but I was a sensitive kid. As long as Brothers and Sisters at the Kingdom Hall kept smiling and complimenting me on it, I would continue to oblige. Dave looked very proud of himself, momentarily. When he realized no one else was laughing, he cackled nervously and adjusted his camo hunting cap. Jenny broke her tranced stare and started to giggle. I felt my bowels start to lose grip. My mother, bless her heart, smirked at Dave in a way that cut right through him like a hot knife through butter. The grin dropped from his face and he slowly backed away, terrified of the look coming from my mother. I stood in locked stare with Jenny sharing equal parts of shock. My face turned from white to red. My mother, as rigid as tungsten, turned to Jenny.

"Is your mother home?" She asked.

Townsend

Jenny's mother politely declined our magazines and Service that day came to an end. The weekend ended too soon and again I was sat back in my fourth-grade classroom. Jenny was staring at me. I had tried my best not to make eye contact with her all morning but after a while she whittled me down and I gave in. She alerted Angie that they had gained my attention, and they both proceeded to point and laugh at me. I had hoped for more from Jenny and for the first time ever, I was disappointed by a girl.

"Do you want to play kickball?" A boy named Gabe asked from a neighboring desk. Gabe was a kid who managed to pull off the Goth look at ten-years-old. He may well have been one of the Goth pioneers in Penn Manor School District. I smiled, nodded excitedly, and ran out of the room as the recess bell rang.

"Hey cool! Your sneakers light up!" I yelled after Gabe.

"I hate them," Gabe responded in a monotone voice.

CHAPTER TWO

No Friends of the World

We always ate dinner as a family, sometimes in the kitchen, sometimes in the dining room. This time it was in the kitchen, at the island in the middle of the room. All four of us sat on bar stools around the green laminate countertop. My father, as customary, prayed over our dinner. As customary I ignored my hunger and pretended to soak the prayer in after he was finished, giving it a few seconds before digging in. Experience. Everything inside my little being just wanted to please my parents. I sought their approval in everything I did. Their validation was almost a drug to me, I craved that release of oxytocin when my parents showed their pride in me; it was crushing when all I achieved was the opposite.

"Hey Dad, I made a friend at school today… his name is Gabe," I told my father. I was excited about it, but I tried my best to sound nonchalant. I wasn't exactly raking in friends at school- for some reason.

My dad looked up at the ceiling, and my heart dropped. That was not the immediate congratulatory response I expected. I realized as he was staring off into heaven that he was trying to place the name and could not. When he realized the name was not on the JW roster, his gaze lowered to me, and he placed his fork down on the table.

"You made a friend at school? No, Jason. You made an acquaintance. We don't make friends with the world. Gabe… is *worldly*." my Dad said as if it were a statement about right and wrong.

I lost my appetite.

"Yes sir," I told my father, pouting into my dinner.

I pushed a green bean across my plate.

"Eat your green beans, honey," my mother said in a rebounding upbeat tone. I guess she was trying to rescue a situation she saw going quickly awry.

WORLDLY

"So, *who* am I supposed to be friends with Dad?" I said, continuing to press my father.

My father matched my mother's positive tone this time, "There are *plenty* of kids your age at the Hall... what about Jamal? There are three Kingdom Halls in Lancaster. Lancaster City alone hosts three separate congregations, bud. Don't *any* of them go to your school?"

"I don't know... I don't think so," I groaned under my breath. My only agenda was to hear it would be alright to be friends with Gabe, but that clearly was not going to happen.

"What, you's don't like the same stuff?" my dad asked.

"Yeah," I said., "He's into, you know... Will Smith and stuff."

"You LOVE Will Smith!" my mother shouted at me and I jumped in my barstool.

She was right. Will Smith was "the bomb" back then, but unfortunately a little *too* cool for me. I felt like Will Smith on the inside but *Carlton* on the outside, the part everyone else

Townsend

sees. Anyway, I decided I had better start cheering up and stop pressing my luck, so I grinned and nodded in agreement.

"I think you mean because he's African American," my dad spouted in a stern tone that caught me off guard.

I tightened up. The accusation cut through me and I responded sheepishly, "N-no way, Dad."

"Look Jason. Jamal loves Jehovah. That is the most important thing and you two have that in common. Talk about Bible stories. Talk about Noah," Dad said.

I gave him a blank stare; I had no words for the man. I was ten, and he thought a friendly conversation starter with other ten-year-old fellas was *Noah and the friggin' animals?*

"You should have friends that like different things..." my dad started.

I thought to myself, *yea right, Gabe likes different things. I guess that is too different.*

"...and we are lucky to have a family of black Brothers and Sisters in our congregation. Congregations in Lancaster

County aren't as diverse as other places. Jamal is your Brother," Dad finished.

Ever since I was a little kid I have thought what a bland world this would be if every flower was the same color. I knew deep in my soul that one of life's great pleasures lies in our differences. *That* was a clear topic of right and wrong. I would not then or ever want to live in a world without that spectrum and I found it irritating that my father even went down that road. Those kinds of values would stick with me and shape my life, just not as he had hoped.

He was preaching to the choir, he really was. I wanted to be friends with Jamal and I craved input. I loved the movie *Short Circuit* and felt like a human Johnny Five. I was drawn to anything different and new. My father knew this and was in a constant battle to keep my curiosity within the lines. Interracial marriages in my world were practically encouraged and I looked at anything different as something I wanted to know more about. The problem in this situation was that I lived in the middle of country nowhere, and there were about maybe ten black people I had ever even *seen.*

Townsend

"If you are going to Bethel one day you will have lots of friends from all over the world!" my mom cheered.

This may require some explanation if you have never heard of Bethel.

***

Bethel was the headquarters of the Jehovah's Witnesses. You can see it in many movies, living room portraits and Jay-Z music videos. You have probably seen it in person if you have ever visited New York City. Have you ever seen the Brooklyn/Manhattan Bridge? Then you have seen Bethel. Go ahead, look it up. Look at the Brooklyn skyline and you will notice a tall building bearing a large sign that says "WATCHTOWER". You may also notice a castle-esque watchtower at the peak, minus an archer. Thousands of people have commuted past this building every day and have never known the amazing story behind it. I (with no ulterior or biased motive) will share.

WORLDLY

In the late 1800s a Pennsylvania man named Charles Taze Russell was forming a new group of Christians that he called The Bible Students. I even have a dopey cousin named after the guy. This group of malcontent Christians was finding holes in their respective conventional religions and was not originally looking to make one of their own. It started as a debate. Russell hosted a popular radio show in which he publicly debated doctrine and his views resonated with a growing group of people. The number of 'Russelites' grew, and they experienced a problem that every religion, sect, and cult face at some point or another...organization.

So, a movement of rebels in theological doctrine needed to adapt. In any example of organization (even in your closet) rules are required. When you set rules, you start to form your own system. His system started in Pennsylvania as Zion's Watchtower Bible and Tract Society and it included roughly fifty-thousand people. Russell had success in publishing a journal called Zion's Watch Tower and Herald of Christ's Presence along with numerous articles in newspapers. Where could he have more success in spreading printed word via newspaper and pamphlets? New York.

Townsend

Russell moved the headquarters and printing operation to Brooklyn, New York in 1908. After his death almost ten years later his successor, Joseph Rutherford (who was also a law man) took over and changed a lot of things. This upset some people causing many to leave and branching The Bible Student movement into four separate groups that went their own ways. Rutherford changed the name The Bible Students to *Jehovah's Witnesses*, the Zion's Watch Tower and Herald of Christ's Presence to *The Watchtower*, named houses of worship *Kingdom Halls,* and insisted on what he called "theocracy" (in JW context, mandatory preaching). Sound familiar yet? Branding.

The distinct changes made a clear brand and Rutherford made it possible for a religion. After all, if you are trying to recruit vast numbers of people for anything, they are going to need to know what you are for, and the more organized you are the better. Law-man Rutherford took a rebellious movement of Bible students, made some rules and turned it into a religion.

That is what Brooklyn Bethel was (until 2016). It was the headquarters, the printing press, the example. It was not just any little printing press running off afterthoughts. It was highly organized. It was Willy Wonka and the Bible Factory, and it was every kid's dream to be an Oomph Loompa, including me. The buildings they bought grew tall and wide as they expanded and bought other properties. Several giant buildings linked together by skyway and underground tunnels. It was a *self-supported community*. A thousand volunteers would spend an average of four years living in small Bethel apartments and working assignments ranging from printing press operators, to cooks, to maids, to illustrators. Much of the food was shipped in from their own commercial-scale farm operation in New Jersey. When I was a kid it was my dream to go to the big city (being no part of the city itself) and go work the Bethel printing presses in Brooklyn… as a writer.

***

"It's not because he's Black!" I hollered in frustration.

My mother slowly turned her head, staring daggers in to me. I calmed my tone.

Townsend

"Geez. He doesn't even like me, OK? He's one of the cool kids," I said, feeling bad for myself. Everyone was stumped, briefly.

"He hangs out with that Chucky Fry, doesn't he?" my dad asked.

I scoffed, "Yea. Chucky Fry".

"That Chucky Fry is going to end up with a career at Weiss Markets pushing a broom! These no-good Gen X'ers, I swear… and their X-games," my father growled.

I wondered why that was a bad thing, those are the kind of jobs you get when you choose a religious education over a college education.

"*OH SUGAR!*" my mother cried, offended by my father's foul language. He was a real Richard Pryor.

"He's ten." I said, now sticking up for Chucky.

When you start busting out words like "dang" in my house it's time to step back and evaluate your position. Things were getting serious.

WORLDLY

"He doesn't go out preaching in service. He stays at home and lets his brain rot. He sits around watching Saturday morning cartoons like "Ren and Stimpy" with his dis-fellowshipped father. He should be doing the right thing and following his mother's example, preaching door-to-door," my dad ranted.

"Greg Long!" my mother's cheerful voice came to the rescue. "He's in Ms. Baumgartner's class. Who knows? Maybe you'll have the same class next year. I'll talk to the principal."

My mother had a grin on her face as she proudly forked a piece of turkey to her mouth.

"I think they like me there, at your school," she finished.

"No…mom..." I discouraged her as I began to feel a panic attack coming on.

"Eat your green beans," she spouted sternly and put me back in my place.

I loved my mother. I still do. My mother worked cleaning houses while my father was the primary bread winner. He

Townsend

worked estimating asbestos abatement after dropping out of college, majoring in calculus. To this day, about the most unexciting lineup of titles I can think of. My father taught us that your job does not have to be enjoyed. Putting too much effort in to school and work is to take equal parts of effort away from the only thing that really matters- God's work. I was discouraged from continuing education and while I was in the public-school system, discouraged from public-school friends.

There was a knock at the front door. My dad put his fork down, squared his shoulders and got up to answer the door. My mother, Louise and I sat quietly. We looked to my father who appeared disgruntled by the intrusion. This man very strongly discouraged contact with the outside world. He did not like worldly visitors. You know... people you don't know, coming up to the front door... uninvited... funny, eh?

I heard my father and a younger voice I did not immediately recognize, shouting in the doorway. There were a few hostile words exchanged before I heard violent sounds of struggle coming from the foyer. Without even thinking I got up and bolted to the front door despite my mother frantically reaching to stop me.

WORLDLY

"Jason! Sit *down!*" my mother scolded while she sat stiffly at the dinner table, refusing to get up.

I ignored her out of instinct. It was not curiosity that drove me to see what was happening, it was love for my father. My socks skid around the corner and stopped in dead shock as I saw my father on the ground, wrestling someone and winning. I looked in the eyes of an eighteen-year-old face that my father was smashing into the foyer rug.

It was my brother, Brett. He is eight years older, and there is a good reason I haven't mentioned much of him. My brother was a full-grown adult. He played such a small part in my life that when coloring in our family tree at school, I'd forget about him and leave him out. My mother would remind me later and I would have to add him as an apple or something. Brett the Apple fell *far* from the tree.

My brother decided a long time ago (when I was a toddler) that he was not interested in the family religion. My parents were not going to make this choice of free will easy for him. Therefore, his time in the Miller home was spent as an outcast. He lived in the basement which had its own entrance and he slept on a couch. Brett came and went as he

Townsend

pleased and for multiple reasons I hardly ever saw him. He was not even allowed at the dinner table. The first and more implicit reason I never saw my own brother was because my parents would not allow it, even when he lived under the same roof. He was basically exiled to the basement after an undoubtedly apocalyptic argument between him and my father, an argument I was too young to recall.

The second and less true reason is that Brett was not all that interested in spending time with his younger siblings. He was a young adult, struggling to be accepted among his peers, and my sister and I were busy eating crayons.

I looked at my brother's face, pressed into the floor and felt excited to just to see him. I guess I took what I could get. I wanted to have an older brother, I wanted to know him. I felt like the older brother, not a middle child. Brett looked up at me and kind of smiled. My father looked up at me also, and with a slight degree of embarrassment, stopped fighting my brother. They both got back on their feet and Brett took the opportunity to shove my father, who almost lost his balance. He clumsily shoved back. I thought it was funny and let a giggle slip through. My father darted a death look my way and I shut up, embarrassed by my indiscretion.

WORLDLY

"I'm just back to get my shit. Fuck off," my brother growled at my father.

Those curse words, as I expected, pierced through my father and boiled his blood. Brett shouldered past my dad and forcibly continued into our home. His demeanor changed immediately when he entered my proximity. Brett reached down and rustled my hair, giving me the kindest smile, I had ever received from him. Maybe he was troubled by what I had just witnessed. I was over it. I was just happy to see him and wanted to play.

"Hey little buddy," Brett greeted me.

"Don't touch or talk to him ya' piece of sh...sugar," my dad scolded, sounding winded, on the verge of hyperventilating.

I cocked my head like a dog, confused at my dad's botched attempt at cursing. My brother walked past me. I turned and watched longingly after him, as my father intently pursued. This is what happened when you made friends with the worldly in my house. My brother made friends at school and did the unthinkable; he went to Spring Break. That was

Townsend

the last straw. My father kicked his eighteen-year-old ass out that day. For the purposes of this story, that was the last time I saw my brother.

CHAPTER THREE

The Devil's Filth

I remember that awful smell of mothballs. The finest house of my childhood reeked of mothballs. It was owned by a fifty-year-old 'bachelor' with a taste for large house plants and oxidized copper statues of naked men. My mother scored a job cleaning this guy's house and it seemed meaningless. Every time we went there it never seemed a damn thing was out of place.

Yet, there was my Mom, sneezing uncontrollably while spritzing various semi-caustic solutions around like mad. Why she picked house cleaning as a part-time job I would never know. She was allergic to everything. She was frail and always sick from something. She couldn't have MSG. Onions in her stomach worked about as well as a fork in a garbage disposal. She once had hay fever and sneezed and coughed so hard she broke a rib. The rib punctured and eventually collapsed her lung.

None of my mother's ailments affected her work ethic. She never missed a house cleaning. Only a handful of times can I recall her ever missing a meeting. My sister and I would go to work with her and try to help make her load a little lighter, but we were kids and easily distracted. I remember one day at the bachelor's house taking a break and ducking into his den downstairs. My sister was old enough to help and she must have been off cleaning one of two-thousand mirrors. In his den I opened a double-door closet and gazed in amazement at hundreds of VHS tapes. I loved seeing them, admiring the pictures on the jackets.

At home the only VHS movies we had were recorded from The Disney Channel free-previews. Once a year we got to scour through TV Guide and request the timer be set to record our annual batch of new movies. Only one time did I convince my parents to spring and buy us a movie, *Dennis the Menace*, starring Walter Matthau. That movie came in a thick plastic cover that opened like a book and I admired its authenticity the whole way home. This was more exciting than generic VHS tapes with four different hand-written movie

WORLDLY

titles. I ran to the VCR to pop it in… and it was blank- so ended our family's movie buying history.

I stared in awe at that man's movie collection. I ran my hand over them like books in a library, and my finger fell on a particular tape in a black jacket. The tape read "Freddie Mercury Tribute Concert". I pulled the tape from its alphabetical order, put it in the VCR and turned on the big screen. I had a biblical moment as I watched James Hetfield, clad in black jeans, a black shirt, black wrist bands and long hair walk confidently onto a stage in front of seventy-two-thousand ecstatic people. This moment left an impression on me greater than any before and became a benchmark in my young life. Watching this new band and new *kind of music*, touched my core ten-fold over any religious presentation to date. It boggled my mind how these men had come so far in their lives. A wave of energy came over my body, and my mind was overrun with excitement. I was bouncing off the walls when my mother charged down the stairs screaming.

"What the HELL is *that*?" she screamed.

I was now jumping out of fear. This was the only time I had ever heard my mother curse. In my house, using the word "crap" made you subject to corporal punishment. I guess I really blew it. I fumbled to pull the VHS out of the VCR. My mother firmly grabbed my wrist and plucked the tape from my hand. Her face was beet red.

"Do NOT let me catch you watching that CRAP ever again, JASON! *Ever!* Satan's filth! You are just begging to be possessed by demons, aren't you?" she hollered at me so hard her voice cracked.

Once she had gotten that out of her system she calmed down a bit, or maybe she smelled the shit in my pants. She looked over the VHS collection and pulled out Willy Wonka and the Chocolate Factory. She quickly stuffed the Freddie Mercury Tribute Concert tape back in its place as if it was crawling with red-eyed satanic roaches.

"If you really need to watch the boob tube Jason, you can watch this," she said, still irritated, but regretful.

My mother trudged up the stairs. I turned to make sure she had left before staring back at the collection. I guess I was wrong and she was still standing at the top of the stair case.

WORLDLY

"Remember Lot's wife, Jason? She looked back too, and what happened to her?" she yelled down the stairs.

I looked at the floor in temporary irritated defiance.

"What *happened*, Jason?" she persisted.

"She turned in to a pillar of salt," I moaned in monotone.

"You should study the Watchtower for Sunday if you're not going to help me clean," she scolded and stomped away.

***

I was twelve-years-old and again sitting in a hallway. This time I was not alone; I was with Greg Long, another Witness. We both sat with our back against the painted block wall and ate our non-Christmas Christmas snacks. We were almost deaf to the classroom party at our backs.

"So, what famous people do you think Jehovah will let into

Townsend

The New World?" I asked Greg while we munched on our snacks.

In my upbringing as an exclusivist Jehovah's Witness, like so many other religions, I was taught that *we* were God's chosen people, that we had the Golden Ticket. I was told that we happened to be the only religion that got it exactly right and therefore the only religion guaranteed to inherit The New World (paradise on earth). With all the Christian variations it kind of seemed like getting a guacamole recipe right, it may taste a little different than someone else's and have a bit more lemon, but it is still guacamole. This exclusivist notion gave me problems even in my prepubescence. As an American I have seen this type of human behavior before, often the general attitude of many untraveled Americans, that we are somehow the sovereign country and despite all the older governments, we got it just right. Sure, America is a great place to live, but I would not want to live in a world without the variety of other countries, our roots. So, I chose to dwell on all the complicated loopholes that the Governing Body (Jehovah's Witness rule-makers) explained that allowed certain unwitting sinners to be granted a pass.

"I think Chris Farley will be resurrected. I want to teach him about The Truth," Greg answered.

"Really? You think Chris Farley will make it? Wasn't he into drugs and hookers and stuff?" I asked.

"Yeah, but he had a Jehovah's Witness heart man. He wanted to make everyone laugh. He was a loving guy… and he didn't know about The Truth, he got dragged too deep into The World. What about you? Who would you study with?"

"Umm… Prince. When I get to study with Prince in The New World, to him *I'll* be the rock star."

"PSH! No way Prince would ever be a J-Dub, he's not gonna' make it!" Greg scoffed.

"You want to hang out after school? I can ride my bike to your house," I asked, hopeful he would accept the offer.

"Man… I live like ten miles away," Greg responded, lacking enthusiasm.

"Yea I know, but I really need to get out," I pled mildly.

Townsend

Greg took a bite of his Snickers bar and drank from his plastic bottle of Turkey Hill Iced Tea before answering me. The classroom party grew louder.

"I wish they'd shut the fuck up, those lemmings," Greg complained.

I was shocked that Greg had used such language. I was more shocked at how good it sounded, he was a natural. I tried to play it cool.

"I can make them all shut up, real f-fuckin' quick," I stuttered over the curse word, but it was passable.

"Yeah? How?" Greg asked.

"Tell them there's no damn Santa," I snarled.

Greg laughed and spit out a peanut from his Snickers.

"They're twelve! Do they still believe in Santa?" he laughed.

"Lemmings will believe in anything," I replied, oblivious to the irony of my statement.

WORLDLY

Greg took the last bite of his snack, smiled and shrugged at me.

"Yeah, come over after school man."

On most occasions I liked being at school. I liked being around other kids my age. That day however I was anxious for the day to end and the whole bus ride home I gathered mental fortitude. After the school bus dropped me off I raced past my sister, sprinting up our quarter-mile long driveway. That day I had places to be, a new friend to make.

We lived on a large property, but it is only half of the original lot. My dad had purposely bought this property from another Jehovah's Witness family. Further up the hill, past another acre of woods, was the McMullen family. The McMullen's have a boy only a year older than me named Mark. Upon buying the wooded property from the McMullen's, building our house there and moving us in when I was little, my parents were optimistic. I would be reared with the path of least resistance leading right to another Witness front door. Mark was prearranged to be my best friend, but it didn't really work out. What my parents did not count on was the fact that his whole family was weird and a little obnoxious.

Townsend

For years my dad tried to encourage me to hang out with Mark. Mark had a high-pitched nasally voice that could be heard for miles. One night at dusk I even mistook a McMullen goat for Mark. I had three-quarters of a conversation with a goat until my sister caught me. She still has not let that one go. After that voice of his interrupted my dad's Bible studies a few times, my obligation to socialize with him started to diminish. It was not until Mark's father came down offering a little too much opinion on where my father should place our blackberry brambles that I was completely relieved of pressure to be friends.

From day one, Mark's preoccupation with having the alpha position in the friendship annoyed me, he felt it was automatically warranted due to his being a year older. It would not have bothered me so much if it were not for the fact that it seemed to be the only thing Mark thought about when I was in his presence. It felt like work to hang out with the kid and was kind of exhausting. We could only do what *he* suggested, anything I suggested to do was always quickly dismissed. Any story I tried to share was interrupted and replaced with one of his (which of course was always 10 percent better).

WORLDLY

I was grateful for the opportunity to make another acceptable (Jehovah's Witness) friend in Greg. My excited sprint up the driveway slowed once I reached my house and saw Mark waiting for me. The smile dropped from my face and my run turned into a wary-paced jog.

"Hey you wanna' ride bikes?" Mark asked me as I jogged passed him.

I fetched my bike from the garage, waiting a moment to answer Mark. Mark perked up when I exited the garage with my bicycle.

"Tell Mom I'm going to Greg's!" I shouted to my sister.

"Sorry, man. I gotta' go," I told Mark and his face dropped.

"Can I come?" I heard Mark say from behind me and I chose to act like I did not hear him.

I could picture it, I bring Mark to Greg's and Greg would never talk to me again. Mark would show up at Greg's house expecting to run the show and I would never get a chance to speak or tell one story, nor would Greg. My sister saw Mark standing there and her face dropped to immediate irritation.

"What? That's like ten miles…" she shouted back in confusion. I didn't stick around to explain any further.

I pedaled my bike a long way up and down sunny country roads. At about four miles I had even passed Gabe. I waved to him, but he ignored me. Even Goth Gabe was cooler than me at this point. I passed an Amish farm and scared a couple of Amish girls on scooters while racing down a large hill. I tried to dodge road apples at thirty miles-per-hour. At the end of the farm I passed a one-room school house where a couple of younger Amish boys stood. They waved, and I ignored them, falsely under the impression that I was at least cooler than *them*. The downhill fun was soon over, the last and hardest part of the journey had come- a mile-long steep hill on top of which Greg's house sat.

I knocked on Greg's door drenched in sweat and panting. Greg answered and let me in. He was shocked by my appearance and probably a little freaked out by the amount of effort I had made to get there. It was quickly apparent that we were home alone, something that would never have happened in my house.

"So… uh, are you cool, man? If I show you something are the Elders going to find out? You won't tell your dad, will you?" Greg asked once we had settled inside.

I tightened up, a bit nervous about what the hell he was gearing up to.

"Yeah… I guess so. Hey… you want to toss the baseball or somethin'?" I asked, turning around in an attempt to get out of whatever trouble he was trying to get me in to.

Greg ignored me and continued, "Have you heard Green Day?".

I hadn't really. Maybe on the school bus radio but hardly recognizable. The cult I was part of worked by deep mental conditioning. Your conscience works as a prison cell to the point that a devout JW will actually tell on themselves if they do something against the rules. JW's are very careful what music they choose to listen to and what movies they watch. My parents were on the extreme side, G-rated movies such as Aladdin and The Smurfs didn't even make the cut. I once went

Townsend

on a school field trip to see Ace Ventura: *When Nature Calls* but my mother came to chaperone. Within the first fifteen minutes of the movie, when the raccoon fell from the tight rope, my mother had enough, and I was pulled out of the theater in front of my whole class.

"Music, man. Rock music. It's the *bomb*." Greg showed off his worldly knowledge.

"D-dope. Put it on," I responded, trying to sound cool and failing miserably.

"What do you think a boob feels like?" I asked.

This was the pressing question that was plaguing my mind at the time. I thought about it constantly. Milk cartons at my school had been replaced with milk bags. There is an unwritten rule within the school system making it a chore to drink milk. The milk bag was not much easier to tap in to than the milk carton; you had to squeeze the bag to firm it up and then stab a pointed straw in to it, praying it wouldn't pop in your face.

WORLDLY

"You think maybe a boob feels like a thing of milk from the cafeteria?" I questioned further.

Greg stopped what he was doing and thought for a moment. I think he had also been regularly pondering the female body.

"I mean I guess that would make sense…" Greg said, thinking hard about it.

"…well those are ice cold, so maybe if she was dead," he guessed.

I made a face and recoiled at the thought. I briefly considered smuggling home a bag of milk and heating it to body temperature in the microwave. Sheltered boys in puberty have a habit of looking for weird substitutes.

Greg put a cassette tape in the family stereo. The opening guitars from *When I Come Around* sent chills up my spine. The chunky muted power chords blasted out of big tower speakers on either side their entertainment center. I was diggin' it indeed. Greg jumped around playing air guitar and I had a seizure (I was going for drums). I guess I was getting a little rowdy because Greg was getting nervous the more excited I got. I began to run around and drum on every horizontal surface. By the time the bridge came in I was temporarily insane and had knocked over one of the tower speakers. The music stopped.

"Dude! What was that?" Greg scolded with the stereo volume knob still in hand.

"I really like that, man... I don't know. I can't really listen to anything like that at my house," I panted.

"Your parents don't let you listen to rock?" Greg asked.

"Johnny Rivers... that's about it. I'm not even allowed to be home alone, man."

True story. In my entire time at that house, I was never left alone once... for fear of what the devil may make me do. I may have even found my sinful penis.

"Who's that?" Greg asked, looking confused.

"It's my dad's favorite... I don't know, like... Oldies. It's OK. I like it," I mumbled.

WORLDLY

"Well. Your family is strict because your dad is an Elder. He scares me dude. Hey! You're not going to tell your dad anything right?" Greg asked with sudden grave concern.

This may require some clarification. Yes, my father served as an Elder in our congregation. The Jehovah's Witnesses do not have a single priest or minister that governs a congregation. It has a "Body of Elders". This was to avoid the corruption of too much power in one man's hands (although the body of Elders still has a "Presiding Overseer"). There is still a head holy honcho and it to this day will never be a woman. Women do not hold any positions of leadership within the congregation that require giving any direction to a male. I remember "auxiliary pioneering" (knocking on doors for a required fifty hours a month, "regular pioneers" are required eighty) on one summer vacation. I took on the "privilege" at the young age of thirteen. The more you did, especially at a young age, the more you garnered favor among the devout adults.

It was a Wednesday morning and the men were all working. I was the only male in attendance amongst the group of females that met to go out in "service". Being the only male, I had to lead the group that morning. My mother, the

Townsend

Elder's wife, had covered her head and started the meeting in lieu of a man, but her conscience quickly caused her to ask me to take over. At thirteen I was most fit to read the day's passage from their daily book of rhetoric called "The Daily Text" to a group of women aged thirty to sixty. The Text was a daily passage of about three-hundred words that included a scripture and an inspirational analysis made to make a two-thousand-year-old book appear relatable. It is required to be read at the start of the day, commonly at the breakfast table. Afterwards we went over the magazines we were presenting that day. I asked for suggestions and points to mention from my audience, picking a raised hand to answer. I asked who would like to drive and organized the carpool groups. I put myself in my own car with my mother; after all, she would have to drive it. I assigned two other women to join us although I would have preferred going without them. In this situation I, a thirteen-year-old boy, had authority over my Mom.

I was advanced in the congregation for my age. I was baptized young, at twelve years old. I auxiliary pioneered (they would capitalize, I will not). I gave talks to the congregation. I answered questions just the right amount at meetings and with just enough content (on Sunday they all read the Watchtower together and the audience answered the questions). Most kids my age were not as enthusiastic as I was in faith yet, but I was an Elder's son. This pretty much made me a preacher's son. On top of that, my father was one of the most rigid men in the congregation. The only kids who were more anal retentive than me were the Presiding Overseer's kids. This caused a more relaxed kid like Greg to be wary of me. The problem was that I had always just wanted to fit in, but anything I have ever done, I have done balls-to-the-wall. I took all those positions as young as I could because it made my dad and the Elders happy, so I wanted to be the best at them. I did not consider how it alienated me from my peers. The older I got, the more curious I was about just being a normal kid, because that was alien to me. I thought Greg was cooler than me because he knew things I didn't about just being a normal kid. His parents were Jehovah's Witnesses too but held no leadership positions, so they were a bit easier going than mine were.

I paused and gave Greg a stupid look. If I told my father that I was over at Greg Long's house, unsupervised and listening to worldly music… I would kick my own ass. A light bulb went off in my head.

Townsend

"Hey, do you have any Metallica?" I asked enthusiastically.

Greg looked around at the kicked-over speaker and the mess I had made. He slowly shook his head.

"Fresh out."

***

By the time I pedaled all the way home I was feeling bad for Mark. I felt horrible that I did not want him to come along to Greg's house, even if it would have been a total disaster. I did not only feel bad that I had not invited him, I felt bad about the way I saw Mark. It was not a very righteous way to act. In fact, it seemed the kind of thing a worldly kid would do. Shutting him out was definitely not what Jesus would do. By the time I pedaled home I was thoroughly exhausted, I had ridden my bike twenty miles to see the second closest Jehovah's Witness kid. Consequently, when I ran in to Mark again I had little resistance to hanging out with him this time.

WORLDLY

Mark must have been watching for me. He 'coincidently' appeared again at the property line when I finally climbed the last hill of our long driveway. My mother must have been doing the same. She came out onto the second story deck that wrapped around the left side of my house to greet me. She failed to notice Mark through the trees.

"Honey, supper's ready," my mother greeted.

I heard a slight twinge of irritation; it was rare that I left the property on my own. It was unusual. I would have to answer Twenty Questions at dinner while my parents probed in to our activities- seeing if I really was where I claimed to be.

"Hi, Sister Miller!" Mark called to my mother.

My mother jumped a bit, startled by the sound of English words coming from a goat's voice. Mom ducked down to peer through the trees. She saw Mark standing on his side of the fence that divided our two properties.

"Oh, why hello there, Mark!" my mother said very sweetly. Only I could detect the hidden lack of enthusiasm in her voice.

Townsend

"I came to invite Jason to dinner with us tonight. Would that be OK?" Mark asked very politely.

My mom was reluctant to answer. Sensing a chance to let the interest in my prior activities fade, I looked up at my mother who glanced back at me. I smiled a dopey, toothy grin.

"Yeah Mom! Can I?" I pled.

My mother gave in. It was much harder to say no to socializing with anyone of the same religion. It was almost a requirement to do so. My religion went to great lengths to distract itself from the fact that its people are isolationists. As if the cult's curriculum did not keep us running in circles enough to forget about the outside world, we also had a social network to deal with within the congregation.

There were congregation basketball games, touch football (tackle only lasted about a year for me until it ended up voted by the Elders as violent, therefore sinful), baseball, roller hockey and sometimes even tennis. These took place of school sports that we were banned from participating in. On top of that, there were large gatherings at public parks and personal homes for wedding anniversaries and graduations-

WORLDLY

the only things not deemed a sin to celebrate. There was a whole social game to play that determined your place in the social hierarchy of the faith. You had to attend the social gatherings and play the right sports. You had to put a ridiculous amount of thought in to how you dress. You wanted to dress trendy enough that the younger kids thought you were attractive, but humble and tidy enough that the adults would not consider you a narcissist or an idolater. You wanted to ride that line between the peers thinking you were cool and the adults thinking you were righteous. The ways to express yourself were vague. It is not like you could join a Slipknot cover band or for that matter even wear the T-shirt. I could not even hang posters on my wall that could be interpreted as idolatry, or I would be accused of worshiping false idols. You had to look harder to see who someone was because the margins were so thin. A kid vying for popularity in a Jehovah's Witness congregation may dress like a golfer in school but break out a fancy suit and tie to impress his real peers at the meetings. A popular JW boy's closet is filled with more fashionable dress clothing for meetings than jeans and T-shirts for school. He will carefully choose his short haircut and keep freshly shaven. Of course, every congregation has its boy who is popular on the merit that he is rebellious and confident enough to not care about it, but Greg had already occupied that spot in my congregation.

Knowing the mental gymnastics that a boy goes through with appearance I could not imagine what a girl goes through. They must always appear modest, skirts below the knees and shoulders covered. They had to carefully appear as if they were modest enough not to care about trends and also to appear modest enough to not be trying to attract male attention. Wearing the wrong skirt could be the cause of a woman ending up in a disciplinary meeting with the Elders, who would be "deeply concerned about her spirituality". Needless to say, Jehovah's Witness dating is a fucking disastrous nightmare (also constantly monitored by nosey Elders).

Mark was the peacock type- with a closet full of carefully-chosen dress clothes for meeting, meant to out dress the other guys. He lived for this shit. It was entirely possible I would be subject to a half hour long explanation of why his belt is superior to every other Brother's. I was willing to except the risk on that day. I needed to scrub my conscience clean of any guilt and perpetuate the lie that existed in Mark's mind- that I liked him.

"OK, honey. Be back by eight-thirty," my mother gave in, letting me hang out with Mark.

"Thanks Mom!"

I ran up the hill and through the woods. I followed Mark home. He immediately burst into thunderous jabber. We ran into his house through the garage. As we ran upstairs the smell of beef stew and woodstove filled my nostrils. It smelled like a New England winter's dinner, but it was not even that cold. Mark's dad was burning off some termite-eaten firewood that had sat around too long. Marks house smelled like a fireplace all year round. I kind of liked it. I said hello to Mark's mom, Sister McMullen, who was still working on the stew in the kitchen. That clued me in that Mark had other pressing business than just dinner. It was not ready yet, as he had alluded to with my mother.

"Come on!" Mark called me to follow him upstairs to his room. We stomped up the wooden stairs to his bedroom.

"Close the door behind you," he whispered.

I carefully closed the door, so his parents could not hear it latch. There were rules in both of our houses that doors stay open for parental monitoring. I sat at the padded one of two wooded chairs in front of Mark's twenty-inch tube television. I reached for and picked up a Sega Genesis controller. Mark pulled a magazine out from under his pillow. I perked up, stretching to see the cover and hoping it was something to do with girls. It was a *Motor Trend* magazine. Mark scurried over with it and plopped down in the seat next to me.

"So, man, you know how these magazines come with those little cards in it…" Mark asked slyly.

"Oh yeah, look the new Subaru, *dude*!" he sidetracked.

"Yeah, yeah… the cards advertising a subscription to other magazines." I said trying to rein him back in.

"Well check *this* one out." he replied.

Mark fumbled through the magazine pages trying to find a thin 3"x5" card bound between the pages. He handed me the magazine. The card read:

Playboy Magazine

Send away for one FREE issue!

WORLDLY

The Sega controller slipped out of my hands and fell to the ground, my jaw bounced off my collar bone and my jowls began to salivate. I stared at the card which even showed a half-inched size sample magazine cover. I squinted to try and make out the image.

"Should I do it?" Mark asked. I think he asked me, so he would have someone to blame if he got caught.

"YES," I replied.

Townsend

CHAPTER FOUR

Sex Education

By the time I was fifteen I went to Greg's house often. I didn't even care for the guy that much, but it was an escape. It's not like I had a lot of options. I was not allowed to be friends with Gabe. We were a secluded group that hardly coexisted with society. Even other devout Christians were a threat to us. I would take blank tapes over to Greg's house, dub copies of his worldly devil music, and rock out. My father searched my room nearly every day looking for contraband that I had stashed. I had to be clever. He found a lot, despite some very extensive measures of concealment. In my later teens I could have been employed by a cartel in smuggling.

In those days kids listened to music on a Walkman, so we used cassette tapes. It was annoying because if you didn't like a song you had to fast forward, hit play, repeat five times until you found the one you wanted. Cassette tapes made it possible for the first generations of music pirates. If you had a double tape deck you could copy tapes (called dubbing). I would dub rock and heavy metal music onto blank tapes and label them things like "Bible Verses", '96 District Assembly", and "Kingdom Hall Music". You get the idea. Believe it or not that incredible plan did not always work, and if I was found out, my ass was grass.

I also had gotten beat with a JCPenney catalog stashed under my bed that had a heavily trafficked bra section. In order to learn what every boy needs to learn about himself, I had to hide. My parents would routinely barge into the room trying to catch me in a sinful act. I did get caught in the act, more than once, and it was intensely shameful and embarrassing. That approach just made me even more curious, and I went to greater lengths to learn about girls. It became a forbidden obsession to see them naked.

Speaking of grass, our family owned a full acre of it. It was my chore to mow the grass which was also my favorite time to listen to my pirated heavy metal. Metallica's *Black Album* and *Master of Puppets* helped my scrawny teenage body push a lawnmower for two hours. I had mowed the lawn enough times (for ten dollars a pop) to buy a mix-matched and heavily-used drum set. That drum set became my desert island. When I was there I was in my own curious world, and I could bang on it.

I would put my headphones on and learn the songs. Unfortunately, my father had also learned the songs as counter-intelligence. One evening as I was blasting into the very distinct opening of *Sad but True* I was suddenly grabbed from behind, my sticks fell to the ground. I screamed in pain as my father sneaked up on me and lifted me off the drum set...by my left ear.

"You're not content with just listening to the Devil's music, huh?" my father screamed in rage. "You have to play along too?

"I knew it! I couldn't sleep last night, Jason! It's this music! There was a demon sitting above your bedroom door!" my mother chimed in screaming hysterically from the garage door. Deputized JW-CIA backup had arrived.

WORLDLY

***

Once again, I had found myself mowing the yard and listening to another mislabeled copy of a Metallica album. This time I tried to play it cool. No bobbing of the head, you never know who is watching from the second-floor windows. It was only a week ago that I had got caught playing along to the Devil's music and I thought I was kind of hiding in plain sight. Surely, I could not be stupid enough to listen to it again when my left ear was still ringing, a disciplinary reminder. No one can fathom the determination of my stupidity- *no one*.

I had mowed about three-quarters of an acre and was on the home stretch, a large open field that was good for tossing the baseball. The edge of the property was lined with sycamore trees and a post-and-rail wooden fence. I saw something moving from beyond the property line that caught my attention. River Road was not busy, and it was not often I saw other people. Today I saw two figures walking down the road- two figures in bikinis.

Townsend

There is a problem with East Coast trees, namely, they are always dropping shit. They drop squirrels, squirrel shit, bird eggs, bird shit, seeds, leaves (in the fall *a lot* of leaves), needles, dead bark, dead branches, acorns and sometimes even bee hives. Pine trees drop pine cones. Pine cones and lawnmowers do not mix, and you know what I mean if you have ever run over one. It makes a terrible sound, almost like a shotgun, that makes your butt pucker.

I hit the world's largest pine cone while trying to be nonchalant and check out the two passing girls. The pine cone sailed through the air and smacked into a tree near them. They jumped like they had heard gunfire and turned back to see what had just happened. I put my red face down and stared in to the chrome handlebar of the lawnmower, pretending I had not seen them or heard them yelp. *Just mind your own business* – I pled with myself – *they'll be gone in a minute.*

No such luck. I finished the line I was mowing and reached the property edge. When eventually forced to, I looked up to turn the lawn mower around and there they were, right in front of me. They were staring directly at me, leaning on my dad's fence, amused at my embarrassment. I pretended to be surprised by their presence and killed the lawnmower.

WORLDLY

"Hey, who are you?" Blue Bikini asked.

"Uhh… Jason Miller. I live here," I stuttered and reluctantly approached the girls.

"How come we don't know you?" Yellow Bikini asked.

I had a feeling these girls were familiar with everyone. They were wet… they must have been swimming in the *crick*. Yellow Bikini snapped her gum and I swallowed nervously. I was taking too long to respond. Maybe she thought I was a little slow. I did not want to tell them the reason they do not know me is because they were not allowed to. I did not want them to know I knew exactly who they were, or that I had spent probably about four hours to-that-date wondering what they looked like in bikinis. I did not want them to know this was kind of a big moment for me. I did not want to tell them about my religion. I did not want to tell them that if my dad saw them he would both call the police for trespassing and then the Elders (the elders to interrogate my filthy mind- I'd rather go with the police.). Yellow snapped her gum again and I snapped out of it.

"Oh, I think you're a grade ahead of me," I bullshitted.

Townsend

"Whose parties do you go to?" Blue Bikini asked.

I was fresh out of bullshit.

"I, uh…I don't go to any parties," I said sounding very unsure of myself.

I was feeling a lump grow in my throat and in my jeans. I couldn't help but look at their perfect bodies. Water dripped from their hair down their goose-bumped breasts and soaked into their bathing suits. They didn't even bring a towel. Shit, the confidence.

"JASON!" my father called from about a hundred yards away.

A normal kid would know from the position of his voice that about eighty trees blocked his view. Not me, I still think my father invented recon drones in the basement just to spy on me- and later sold the patent to the military. The next words I chose were not exactly my best.

"Go… *get*!" I said in a loud whisper as I scurried away.

WORLDLY

The Bikini Girls thought my panic attack was hilarious. They did not take the interruption as serious as I had. They slowly climbed off our fence, with a kind of defiance that I admired.

"Come to Gabe's house tonight! He's having a party!" Blue Bikini shouted.

"Gabe? He hates me! I …can't. I don't have a car," I whispered.

I pulled the rope on the mower as quick as I could, and the mower refused to start. The girls looked insulted.

"Loser!" Blue Bikini snarled.

"Yeah dude, you're a fuckin' loser!" Yellow Bikini concurred, and I pretended not to hear.

"*I hit a dang pine cone*!" I yelled toward the house as I tugged at my pants.

"Mark is here!" my dad yelled back.

Townsend

I felt a bit of relief now that I knew why my dad was hollering for me. I felt a stronger feeling of regret that I had made an ass of myself to the girls and told them to "get". I eventually got the mower to start, finished mowing the final line and tried to forget about the girls… but cursed myself in embarrassment all the while. Exhausted, I dragged the lawnmower up the incline to my dad's garage and met Mark there.

"Hey Jason, you gotta' come play video games man. I just got a new one for the Genesis." Mark said with an air of mischief in his voice.

"Yea? What did you get?" I asked him as I hosed the cakes of grass guts off the mower.

"Jurassic *Park,*" he responded, persisting with the mischievous tone.

I looked up at him, this was an obvious lie. Mark had been pushing that terrible game on me for years. Mark gave me an exaggerated wink. Even he automatically knew there was a possibility our conversation was being monitored. Shit, it was probably no safer at his house. My interest piqued.

WORLDLY

"Yea, OK man," I responded to Mark.

"Supper's ready!" my mother called from the kitchen.

"After dinner, alright?" I asked, and he nodded.

I sat at the dinner table and lowered my head as my father said a prayer over the meal. When he finished, I geared up for a debate.

"Dad, I was studying earlier, and something just doesn't sit right."

"Yeah? What's that?" my father asked.

"Well, the Amish really think they have it right, right? They think they have the truth... I mean, they gave up electricity for it," I proceeded with caution.

"The Amish ignore large swaths of the Bible that command us to preach to others. They do the opposite and seclude themselves," my father cut in.

"Ok. Um, we definitely don't do that..." I mumbled sarcastically.

Townsend

"The Catholics…" I began, mowing over my remark.

My father scoffed and nearly spit a pea across the room.

"The Catholics think *they* have it right. Well, they've been around a lot longer then we have," I continued.

"A lot of them are thugs who do it out of ritual. They believe in the Trinity. They took God's name out of the Bible. Psalms 83:18. They have no personal relationship with Jehovah," my mother chimed in.

"Let him speak," my father scolded.

My mother lowered her head and looked at her food.

"The Jews, they were around before the Catholics even. Jesus was a Jew. They've been persecuted more than we have," I said.

"They killed Jesus," my father responded solemnly.

I was at a loss for words. What I was fighting was a feeling, almost a moral quandary deep inside that was hard to verbalize and I was not articulate enough to relay it. My parent's greatest education was in arguing the Bible. I had no chance, not even a prayer.

"There are as many false religions as there are fish in the sea, Jason. Jesus said, 'The path is narrow…'. The Jews and Muslims also slaughter each other over scraps of land, long after anything holy happened there," my father continued.

"It's just that these people can't help it," I said.

This kind of resonated with them. They did feel compassion for other human beings and this notion got to them… pity. If devout Christians don't hate contrary believers, then they at least pity them. It's only natural when you are face to face with someone you believe is doomed. To us, preaching door-to-door was like walking down the cancer wing of Lancaster General Hospital.

"That's why we preach," my father stated.

He paused. He wanted me to go on and snatch for more rope to hang myself with.

"They think, no, they *believe* they are doing the right thing… that they have it right. So, God is going to let them all die and miss out on paradise because they got it wrong... on a technicality? It just doesn't sit well with me," I said.

My father lowered his fork and tongued his teeth, thinking a moment.

"It all really comes down to this, Jason. None of these religions follow Jesus's commandment to spread his word before the end comes. Armageddon is mentioned in the second book of the Bible along with Jesus's commands. In fact, some of them do the opposite. They seclude themselves from the outside world," my father said.

"We seclude ourselves too," I let slip.

My father slammed his fist on the table.

"I wasn't finished. The Catholics are more corrupt than most dictatorships, they speak for themselves. I mean, they single-handedly tried to rewrite Christianity. The Jews killed Jesus, and although they professed the Messiah would come, chose to ignore it when it happened because it was inconvenient. I mean really, Jason. You're baptized. You've studied the Bible your whole life. We have the truth, that's why it's called The Truth," he preached.

I rolled my eyes; I just could not help it at that point. I wasn't getting the answers I wanted. Nothing he said satisfied me in the least. I just got frustrated and that made me angry.

"If you look at any of these religions it's easy to see that they cherry-pick what they will and will not follow in God's will, the Bible. We don't fight, and we don't kill other human beings. Turn the other cheek. We don't invest ourselves in man's imperfect governments. We trust in God and the Bible and *truly*... follow It," he argued.

"What version of the Bible? What if the Bible is just a book written to control people? It just all seems and sounds so man-made to me. I mean it was just a papyrus book... how convenient. If it came from a creator wouldn't it be permanently written in the sky?" I complained.

My father was growing irritated.

"Matthew 24:14. It's very easy to understand and how many people follow it? Jesus organized his disciples in twos and sent them door-to-door to spread God's word. He never said stop. He said continue until the end comes. How many people have the BALLS to go out and face people, get spit on, laughed at and tormented for just spreading a positive message and trying to save their lives? Jesus was one. We do too. We are not better than Jesus. He came here to show us how to do it, and still, the vast majority ignore it. Very few religions have managed to *not* ignore that simple task. Anyone whose congregation does not try to preach the message is blood guilty, Jason. The path is narrow. You can find some comfort knowing that what we do is not common. You don't want to be Catholic or Muslim and look around and see a quarter of the world claiming to also be Catholic or Muslim with you. That is not a narrow path, Jason. False religion will perish. The Wild Beast will turn on Babylon the Great. Do you want to go down with them or do you want to live forever in paradise on Earth?" he asked.

My dad tried to calm down and furiously forked a green bean in to his mouth. Another thought hit him before he was done chewing. I sat in disgruntled silence.

"The Jew's were persecuted? Two thousand Jehovah's Witnesses were slaughtered by Nazi's... in concentration camps. You don't see that on the History Channel. There aren't countless documentaries made on that subject. No one talks about that, that Jehovah's Witnesses were second most killed to Jews... and you know what? We don't want them to either. The road that's narrow," he continued on.

What I had a problem with, and at the time it was just a suspicion, was the Bible itself. I was having questions about evolution also, but I knew no scientists therefore I knew no one that could give me an answer that I would trust. I knew if I pressed that issue it would be too much like kicking the crutches out. Losing faith in the Bible is pulling Christianity out by the root. Who knows what would happen if I stuck to that argument, it was not safe and therefore it was not smart to go down that road. I will tell you, for someone so concerned about his religious freedom, my father did not appear to be concerned about mine.

"I want to buy a car," I said, probably picking the worst moment in history to bring it up.

My dad slammed his fork down... again. My father wouldn't let me buy my own car, even if it was my own hard-earned money buying it. I had been working since the age of

Townsend

fourteen, mostly as an excuse to get out of the house. I brought home a cordless phone once and he put the corded one back up, so I would remain leashed to the wall and easier to eavesdrop on. He wanted me to use the old family truck because his name was on it, not mine- another leash. My father craved control, but the more he squeezed the more he pushed me right through his fingers.

After dinner I asked for permission to go see Mark. My father groaned and said it was alright as if he was doing me some big favor. Whatever would take the conversation off me buying a car the day I turned sixteen. In Pennsylvania at the time you could even drive at fifteen and a half.

After dinner I headed to Mark's house by way of the woods. I kicked through all the fallen leaves with my Vans sneakers and ducked under low branches as I had hundreds of times before. When I popped out of the woods and onto Marks driveway I made sure to shake out my jeans to not become infested with ticks…again. I heard a riding lawn mower idling unusually fast from afar. Mark put the mower in the fastest gear, six, and was barreling towards me. I stopped right before an opening to a trail that looped through the woods and popped out on the opposite end of their driveway. Mark had blazed that trail in himself with the lawn mower. When he was only feet away it became a game of Chicken. I stood there motionless, trusting that I knew his next move. He tried his best to convince me he was going to run me over with a five-hundred-pound lawn mower. At the last moment he jerked the wheel sending the back tires in a slight skid, kicking up a small amount of gravel and dirt from their driveway, and headed full speed up into the woods. He downshifted into third gear as he entered the trail that continued into the woods and up a hill. It was as if he thought he was driving a dune buggy instead of a twelve horsepower Craftsman lawnmower. Bolts and brackets banged and rattled furiously as he blasted through the self-made trail. It was soon followed by a huge *slam* as the lawn mower sailed over a small "jump" he fashioned. I continued up the driveway in the same direction the lawnmower was through the woods, towards his house. I reached his garage before he did and stood patiently waiting. He took the long route looping around the back of his house before popping out from the side of the garage and skidding to a hard halt.

"Woo! Man, I think I squeezed another half a horsepower out of her," Mark bleated.

Townsend

"Cool man, can I take a spin through the trail?" I asked.

"No way man, that trail is a black diamond, only I can negotiate it. Only I can drive this girl. You can hop on the back though and hang on, though. I'll take you for a ride," Mark said.

That sounded about fifty times more dangerous than what I had asked for.

"It's cool man," I said. "So, what did you do to this thing?"

Mark cleared his throat and walked around to the front of the lawn mower as if he was about to explain cold air forced induction on a Lamborghini.

"Well, as you can see, I took the hood off. Helps keep her cooler and that adds something. If you look over here, I changed the spark plug to a Spitfire. It has three electrodes instead of just one and I made a spark plug wire for it," Mark boasted.

"You *made* a spark plug wire?" I asked.

"Yeah, it came off my dad's Subaru after the last tune up. It was in great condition and I could make it work. The bandwidth on a wire from a car is more optimal."

"It's a lawnmower, Mark. Why don't you ask for a go kart?" I asked, unable to hold back laughter any more.

Mark looked irritated.

"It *is* a go kart! Once the lawnmower deck is removed it's pretty much just a go kart!"

"You removed the deck, now it's just a lawn tractor," I poked at him. It was too funny; he was actually getting upset.

"Naw, it's cool man. I mean, I don't have anything with an engine in it. I'm not allowed to. So at least you have this," I said, diffusing the situation before he sent me home without finding out why he called me to come over. I kicked the chunky back tires.

"D-don't do that!" Mark yelled in a panic, his voice cracked.

Townsend

I dropped my hands to my side and could not hide my irritation anymore.

"OK man, what do you want to do then? You want to play Jurassic Park?" I asked trying to appease him.

Under no circumstances did I want to play that game again. We had played that game through and it was becoming redundant. It was not about the game and he knew that. There was something he was purposely tip-toeing around, and so was I. I was making an excuse to go inside and giving him a chance to tell me the news. The problem was that he knew now that was what I wanted. I was being too impatient. He was going to use the news as a ransom to hold me hostage in the recreational activity of his choosing.

"YEA! Dude so I found a new raptor! It is hidden in level three, but here's the thing- I think it's stronger than the others! With the shotgun it normally takes…"

"Three hits," I interrupted.

"… yea three hits to kill a raptor. *This* one… took *six*."

"Wow." I said unenthusiastically.

"Well I don't know anything for sure. It will need more test runs to know. I wonder if it is a glitch or a..." Mark paused, reluctant to say the next word.

"*Easter egg*," he whispered, looking behind him to make sure no one heard him mention the pagan holiday.

"Yea, maybe."

"An Easter egg is something a designer hid in a game. It has nothing to do with Easter." Mark explained, his conscience eating at him for just saying the word.

"Yeah. I know. It's OK. They could just call it a gift or something, though," I said.

"Wanna' see?" Mark asked, his voice turning up an octave in excitement.

"Sure," I said, giving my best effort to appear excited about it. "Hey, so do we have to play through the first two levels to try to get to that spot in level three?" I asked.

"Yep!" Mark answered, and my heart splattered on the driveway.

Townsend

Once again, we stomped through Mark's house that smelled like a fireplace. We took our shoes off in the foyer and slid across the old oak floors. Mark's mom called to us from the living room. Our pace slowed, and we answered her in the living room.

"Well hello Jason!" Mark's mother cheered. "Are you staying for dinner?"

"Uh…" I thought about how long this information was going to take to drag out of her son. "Yeah… I think so… if that's OK."

"Of course, it is. I'll set another place for you tonight then. What are you boys up to?" she asked.

"Workingonthetractorvideogamesnow, Mom," Mark replied in irritation for the both of us.

"OK then. Leave the door open," his mother answered in a cheery tone. "So, you can hear me when I call for dinner."

We stomped through the house and clattered up the old oak stairs to his bedroom. Mark sat down first, claiming the chair with a cushion before I could. He turned on the Sega and started playing before my butt even hit the chair. Jurassic Park was a one-player game. So, this meant I was to sit there and watch Mark play and die repeatedly until he finally made it through three levels to the spot where he thought there was a special raptor. I was rooting for the raptor.

"I think I prefer the machine gun if I am going to meet this super raptor," he said.

"Cool," I answered, purposely quiet.

I was now playing another game with Mark. He lost his power as soon as we got to his room to play video games. He silently held the news over my head to get me there, but now I had the power if he wanted me to stay and hang out with him. Mark smashed away at the buttons on the controller. He peeked over and saw me slumped in the chair, clearly not having much fun.

"Do you want to play a level?" Mark graciously offered.

"Nah man. I'm good."

Townsend

We sat in silence. I let Mark feel the tense air of boredom creep into the room. I started to squirm in my chair and leaned forward as if I might leave. He finally gave in.

"So, uh, you know tha- shut the door," he began. I perked right up and quietly closed the door, turning the handle so the latch would not make a sound.

"You know that card for a free Playboy?" he whispered.

"Uh-huh." I said trying to play it cool.

"It *worked*."

At fifteen years old, this was the biggest news of the year. Shit, this was in the running for the biggest news of my *life*. I was easily more excited in that moment than I had been for anything all year. Back then with the lack of today's technology it was a lot harder to learn about the female anatomy. My house did not possess the internet. It took a lot of guessing. I really wanted to know some things and Mark now had the answers. The problem was that he had just regained the power. I had to play it cool if I ever hoped to see that Playboy.

WORLDLY

"No way," I said, carefully choosing my words. This was the most optimal response to get him to actually show it to me. Doubt the authenticity versus begging to see it. Bring him to me.

"*Yea-huh*," he defended, still hammering away at the Sega controller.

I sat there in utter excitement. I thought of knocking him out and scouring his room to find it. I decided against it, considering the lengths he no doubt went to hide such contraband. I don't know that I would ever find it. Plus, the other annoying fact was that he was a year older, and I could not take him. Whenever we sparred he always had me by a hair, but maybe if I had the element of surprise...

"Dude! Screw this freakin' game! Dang it! Let's see it!" I said bursting at the seams.

I ripped the controller out of his hands and shoved his shoulder. He scrambled for the controller and quickly hit pause to keep from losing his game. He slowly handed the controller back to me.

Townsend

"OK. Fine, you play. I'll get it, but don't look. If you look you don't get to see."

"Yeah *fine!*" I said, still insanely excited.

I waited for him to leave his seat and then proceeded to play the game in his absence. I kept my word and did not peek but heard him fumbling around near his bed. He pulled something heavy that scraped across the floor; there was some metal jangling and the sound of a lock opening. My heart thumped harder with every beat, pumping blood through my veins so fast that I thought I would pass out. He returned to the seat, I opted to play it cool again. I continued the game for thirty back-breaking seconds, even though I could see the glossy cover in my peripheral vision. Finally, I hit pause and turned to him. My eyes turned as big as dinner plates.

Geri Halliwell looked back at me giving me duck lips. She wore some kind of latex dress that doubled as a British flag. The pun, "Spice It Up" read across the May 1998 edition cover. I marveled at how appropriate it was to me. The Spice Girls had been the subject of many a dream, both day and night. They were everywhere at the time. Sometimes I would sneak and watch the MTV Channel hoping to catch a glimpse of them with the sound on mute, of course. Here was Ginger Spice sitting right next to me, she knew what I wanted. Mark stood between me and that dream though. I sat salivating, possibly drooling at the red, white and blue cover.

I sat there panting like a dog, looking at Mark, then at the Playboy, back at Mark and back at the Playboy. Waiting for him to throw me the treat.

"Look. We have to make a promise, a pact… that we will never, ever show anyone else," he warned in sobering tone.

"Yeah, yeah. Yeah! Of course. A pact." I said with a mouth that was now dry for some reason. My body was doing weird, new and drastic changes by the second.

"Seriously, if either of our parents found out… we'd have to leave the frickin' state. It would ruin our lives, man," he further warned. The thought now returned about knocking him out, I knew where the magazine was located now.

"Dude. I know. My dad's an Elder. I will guard this with my *life*," I appeased.

Townsend

Mark handed me the Playboy. The glossy cover smelled like baseball cards and was as slick as ice. My hands clammed on the cover; they were so sweaty I wondered if they would drip. I carefully opened the first page, a two-page advertisement for cigarettes that showed some guy and his horse. That reduced my heartbeat quite a bit. I was disappointed. I expected light to shine forth and breasts to pop out from everywhere, not a dude smoking cigarettes next to his fucking horse. I turned the page four more times until I reached the table of contents. It felt like standing in the lobby of The MGM Grand on a first visit to Las Vegas and seeing the name in person that had been forever dreamt of. I turned page after page of grueling advertisements, cologne samples and articles about God-knows-what until I finally reached Geri on page sixty-seven. I stared at her standing next to the rest of the Spice Girls all singing on stage. I started to read about her when Mark interrupted.

"What are you doing?" he asked and turned over one more page.

Angels sang, and light broke forth from the pages. This was a new day, for I no longer had to imagine what boobs looked like. I peered in awe at the first nude woman I had ever seen. I was eternally grateful to Geri for doing this for me. My whole body tingled, and my eyes began to water. Mark snatched the magazine out of my hands.

"Alright, that's enough for today," Mark demanded.

That FUCK! He was really going to fucking do it. He was going to hold that magazine hostage for God-knows how long as bait, to get me to watch him play his video games for hours on end. I'd probably get one page a visit. It took me sixty-nine pages to see the first real boob and I was questioning how much there was left to see. I thought about girls all the time and I was uncontrollably curious. I wanted to know a girl so bad. I almost wanted to cry. Maybe he would give it back after half an hour. It was best to stay positive about these things. I was prepared to beg to see more of Ginger Spice.

Mark handed me back the Sega controller and strolled back to his bed, reading the Playboy. He flopped down on his bed. I was still frozen from having seen my first naked woman, and then having her ripped out of my hands, in a state of shock. I took the path of least resistance and hit "START" on the gamepad. I continued to play the game, but all my senses directed behind me, to the bed where Mark lay with my

Townsend

new girlfriend. Mark sat in deafening silence turning page after page, the sound from the unwanted video game breaking through the thick air of hormonal tension. I used the game as a chance to pull myself back together and think. Before long I heard the sound of a belt buckle.

"Hey, don't turn around OK?" Mark asked.

Now shock appeared in a different form. My hands began to shake.

"Uh, OK," I responded, not sure what to do or say next.

A squirt came from a bottle of lotion and I started to squirm in my seat again. This was going terribly wrong. Chills crept up my spinal cord.

"So, I was reading this book on psychology, right?" Mark started.

A sound started that sounded like someone chewing with their mouth open. I tried to ignore it and pretend it was not what I knew it to be.

"Yeah…" I responded.

WORLDLY

"Well this doctor- and she's a doctor right- said it is perfectly normal for a group of guys to sit in a circle and uh… help each other out."

I recoiled at the thought but tried to keep as silent and motionless as possible. I thought of the scene in Jurassic Park where the guy tells the girl not to move a muscle, so the T-Rex can't see them.

"Oh," I said, flabbergasted.

I carefully put the Sega controller down and avoiding Mark's general direction- turned to the bedroom door.

"Hey, I have to go."

"Hey, wait!" Mark yelled.

In one fluid motion I opened the door and closed it behind me, accidently letting it slam a little. I pattered down the wooden stairs and into the kitchen where I struggled to put on my shoes as fast as possible but fell over.

"So, you aren't staying for dinner, Jason?" Mark's mom asked.

Townsend

"Oh…no, I'm sorry Sister McMullen… I forgot I have a test I have to study for!" I replied.

"Well that's one of the benefits of home schooling! Your mom would not let you forget. There is no way Mark would ever forget he had a test coming up," Mark's mom lectured, I wondered why I was getting this pitch now of all times.

"You should have your mom call me. You should really be home schooled, Jason. Public school is no place for a Witness boy. Especially during high school, there is so much going on with the immoral worldly kids nowadays. Generation X has really destroyed any morality left in the world," she lectured on.

"Gotta' go! Thanks for letting me come over! See ya'!" I said running out of their front door.

I ran down that driveway as fast as I could. I had never gotten home so fast from Mark McMullen's house before.

Twenty hours later I came home from school to Mark, his father and my father sitting at the picnic table up on our deck. Mark was worried I would say something and had told on himself. Mark and I sat for over an hour as our fathers lectured us about how immoral pornography was. My father read several scriptures and prayed over us. Thank God, Mark had left out the last detail. I was grounded for two months and had to sleep with my bedroom door open indefinitely... for seeing my first naked woman at fifteen years old.

***

Even though my father forbade me, I bought my own car anyway. At sixteen I had saved up from mowing lawns and washing trucks at a landscaping company. For five-hundred dollars I had bought a 1991 Volkswagen Jetta from a girl at school. It was turd brown, but that ended up being a blessing. It was camouflage. I thought my father would have killed me if he knew I had gone against his wishes and bought my own car, so I hid it in the woods. Whenever I left the house to go to work, my parents assumed I was walking. Ten miles I believe it was to this new job I insisted on having at the hardware store.

Townsend

I would open the door of the car, push it through the woods in neutral, check to make sure the coast was clear, and take off down River Road. That would buy me a significant amount of free time every work day.

I drove my turd-brown Jetta through Conestoga, stopping at a roadside farm stand. These stands are operated by both Amish and regular farmers alike. It's a chance for a farmer to make some side cash under the table, and a chance for the locals to reap the benefits of enduring the fertilizer smell all summer long. I ate well in Lancaster County. I examined a heap of corn ears, selected half a dozen, and continued on my way to Ace Hardware.

At the hardware store I got the tedious job of stock boy. It was a job most of us shared however. I also had to run the register from time to time. At that moment I struggled to find a home for a box of quarter-inch bolts in a sea of hardware.

"My sister says, 'what's up'? Man, did you see that new chick? The cashier? Fuckin' tits out to here man," Dave, my supervisor, greeted.

WORLDLY

This was Dave, brother of Jenny. Jenny was the girl I had run into when I was going door to door for ministry; Dave was the one flicking my Mickey Mouse tie. He was now my boss. He was also currently using two boxes of wax rings for toilets as a visual aid to simulate breasts. I shook my head.

"Jeez man, take it easy," I laughed.

"What are you some kind of Jesus freak, bro?" he mocked, already well aware of the answer.

"I'm Christian, if that makes me a Jesus freak, I guess so."

"Fag," Dave mumbled.

"Redneck," I mumbled back.

Dave had piqued my interest, even though I pretended not to care. He, the shift supervisor, was peaking around the corner of the aisle to get a good look at Meredith, the new girl. I couldn't help it and I joined in, peeking over his shoulder.

Meredith was a well-endowed country girl and as pretty as sunshine. It was sunshine for me at least- Dave was a

Townsend

cloudy day. She stood like a beacon behind the cash register island talking to a male customer who was being overly polite. A line was suddenly beginning to build. At that moment the top of Dave's head looked like a ball of yarn to a cat- so I swatted it. Dave turned around, shoved me into the aisle, and punched my shoulder. Meredith turned to see what the commotion was.

Meredith's voice came over the loudspeaker thirty seconds later, "Cashier to the front please."

Dave stopped scuffling and the grin went grim.

"That's you, bro!" he demanded.

"What? Fuck no, you go!" I insisted.

"I am your manager…" he stated with a serious tone.

"*Shift supervisor,*" I corrected.

"Regardless, I am your boss and Meredith *needs you, bro*. I'm farming this one out," Dave insisted.

WORLDLY

There was no getting out of it... I was trumped. I tossed him the box of quarter-inch bolts that I couldn't find a home for. In about two seconds he had glanced at the tag and put them on the shelf where they belonged. He was free to continue following the spectacle. I hesitated, and he smacked me in the back of my head.

"Go ahead... Jesus! Go tap that ass!" he taunted.

"Dude, shut up. I have a girlfriend."

"Not like that you don't." He taunted further.

"Dude. She's like sixteen. How old are you?"

"Whatever. GO," he answered.

I approached the front of the store and entered the cashier's island housing two cash registers. She turned to me, I had hoped she would just keep doing her job and not say a word to me. Now I had to respond to her in front of a line full of men who probably all wanted to be a sixteen-year-old male cashier right about now... and would rather I be dead.

Townsend

"Hi. I'm Meredith. Thanks for helping," she said. God, her voice was sexy too.

"Yeah... no problem... I'm Jason," I said with a shaky voice.

"He can take the next customer over there,'" Meredith told the line of men.

The men looked at each other, then at me. None of them wanted to give up their place the line they were already in. I expected them to start drawing straws. One guy finally gave in and clomped over to my side. I nervously fumbled on the keys of the cash register trying to type in my employee code. I got it wrong twice. Out of the corner of my eye I noticed Meredith watching me. She raised an eyebrow and smacked her gum again. From the other side of the counter the customer was scowling at me, his eyebrow raised.

After the line of customers was sent on their way Meredith and I took a break. We sighed in relief, as if we had just won a small battle.

"So what school do you go to?" Meredith started.

"Penn Manor. You?" I asked, just glad that she began talking first.

"Manheim," she answered.

"Oh yeah, I thought so. I- I'd probably remember you," I stuttered.

Meredith smiled a big, toothy grin with gum sticking out of the side of her teeth. I turned red. What did I just do?

"Awww. Wow Jason. You're cute," she said playfully.

She was used to being hit on. She handled my obvious slip with skill. She leaned over while she spoke and rubbed her hand down my shirt. I heard a box of bolts fall to the ground in the back of the store.

"Shit!" Dave whispered from afar.

"Nah, I mean... I just remember faces. I- I have a girlfriend."

It was no use. At sixteen you are a wild animal. You do things when you are in puberty you would never do just a few years later. Your brain does not operate on anything but pure high-octane hormones, like running an engine on pure nitrous oxide. Yea you can go like that for a while, but if you go on for too long you are going to blow up, collect a variety of STD's, or ruin your life.

I looked uncomfortable, like I was going to fart. Meredith turned her back to me and returned to her cash register. She opened the register and a check fell to the ground. She backed up until she was about a half of an inch away from me. I stared into her mane of curly blonde hair. I closed my eyes and I could smell her shampoo. Meredith bent over and firmly pressed her bottom into my lap. I kind of jumped without moving away and looked down in amazement. I wondered if I was poking her and if she could feel it. I looked away to tried to think of something else. I glanced out the store window in time to see my father and mother approaching. They were dressed formally.

"Crap!" I yelled.

I carefully slid past Meredith's backside and left the cashiers island, knocking over a bunch of pencils in the process. I opened the front door for my parents.

"Thank you, Son. So, this is what you missed service for today..." my father grumbled.

"I had to work, Dad," I replied courteously as possible.

My mom wasted no time interrogating any female in close proximity to me. This time it was Meredith.

"Hi, I'm Mere. I'm Jason's new girlfriend," Meredith joked.

Meredith popped on her heals making her breasts jump in her tight shirt and stuck her hand out. My mom gave my father a shocked look, and reluctantly offered her hand in return. I caught it while looking up from picking up the fallen pencils.

"Ummmmm…" my mom started to protest.

"I'm kidding! I just started working here, this is my third day," Meredith laughed.

My mom and dad cackled nervously, trying to be polite and wanting to be anything but.

Townsend

"So, do you need a ride home?" Dad asked me.

"Aww, no Dad. Thanks. I still have a whole cart to stock and a few things to clean up after closing," I replied trying to field my Dad's disappointment.

"You need to be studying for the meeting tomorrow," he barked.

"Yeah, I know Dad," I said, beginning to get annoyed.

"No job ever comes before that."

I was beginning to fear a public lecture. Meredith looked over, bewildered.

"Yeah, you're right. So, I better get to finishing up then, right? I'll get a ride home from Dave," I reasoned.

"I don't want you riding with…"

"JASON!" Dave shouted from the back of the store, saving me.

"*Dad*. I have to work, OK?" I pleaded.

WORLDLY

I handed my dad an Ace Hardware pencil as a white-flag peace offering.

"No, thank you. That's stealing."

My parents left the store. My dad scowled back into the store before getting in our car. I was shaken... that was close. If my parents had caught me dry humping Meredith the Worldly in the cash stand of Ace Hardware, I would have been toast. Dave appeared out of thin air right beside me.

"I knew you were a freak. So, I'm driving your ass all the way back to Conestoga tonight, huh?"

About an hour later the store was locked and I headed out to my forbidden VW Jetta. Remember, at this point, my parents have no idea I even owned a car. I kept it parked behind a pallet of plywood, in the stockyard behind the store. I checked on the ears of corn and left for my (extra forbidden) girlfriend's house.

***

Townsend

I parked my car in front of a well-manicured house sat in the middle of a development in Millersville, Pennsylvania. I got out of my car and looked around. I liked it here. I liked developments. They are clean and orderly. I felt like a lot must go on in developments as opposed to living out in the sticks. I walked past their white picket fence and up to their glossy red front door. I did not trip over pine cones or get attacked by any overconfident rodents on the way there.

Yea, the suburbs are nice, I thought.

Once inside, I sat at a dinner table boasting a hearty Italian dinner- including my corn on the cob. Michelle sat beside me, her parents Beverly and Tony sat at either end of the table. Michelle sneakily grabbed my hand under the table. Her eleven-year-old brother, Tim, knew exactly what was going on and taunted us from across the table, pretending to barf in to his plate. I admired the sight of her young and happy parents. They must have been in their late thirties.

"Jason! Thanks for the corn, fella'. What are your plans for school?" Beverly asked with a strong Long Island accent. I wondered if she was laying it on a bit, I loved it either way.

"Umm, I don't really know," I sighed.

Beverly shot Michelle a concerned look.

"My family doesn't really believe in college. I mean unless you're really smart and could be a doctor or something... I guess."

"Whataya frickin' kidding me?" Beverly shouted.

Tony choked on his food and laughed with his wife. I chuckled too, it seemed she was just busting my chops, I was not exactly sure.

"Well, what do you like? What are you interested in?" she continued.

"Well I like stories and writing and I... really like shop class. I like woodworking, electronics, building computers. I like... making stuff," I said, trying to give my best response.

Townsend

No one had ever asked me that question before; I was supposed to go to Bethel. That was the best I could do.

"My father and I are part of the building committee in The Truth."

"The Truth? What the hell is that?" Beverly asked.

"Oh… it's what they call my religion," I answered hesitantly, suddenly aware that it sounded a bit foolish.

Beverly and Tony cracked up laughing but stopped themselves when they realized they may have hurt my feelings.

"I'm sorry, honey. That just seems a little ridiculous, naming a religion 'The Truth'. Maybe we will start a religion and call it "The Truth to Infinity, No Backsies". Go ahead. What are you interested in doing?"

"I have always had a passion for building. In our religion we build our own churches. Everyone gets together, and they just do it. It is very organized. You register your trade, so they know who can do what, and within a week it's done. It's called a Quick Build. In 1998 I got to go to the Virgin Islands with my dad to rebuild a Kingdom Hall that was destroyed in Hurricane Georges. I loved it. Even as a little kid I would watch *New Yankee Workshop* and *This Old House* with my dad. I think I enjoy it even more than he does. I like how things are built," I said.

*

As a side note, I had gotten in a bit of trouble at the Quick Build in the Virgin Islands. I made a friend with a kid my age and we explored the tourist resort that we all stayed at together. One night I got back to the room before my father did.

"They really put the ZING in Ting-Zing here, man," I slobbered when my father entered the room.

Ting is a popular island soda in a green bottle with a yellow label. You can find it in some import stores and bodegas. Zing is booze.

"Are you *drunk?*" my dad growled.

Townsend

"I just tried it! It's OK, Dad! There's no drinking age here," I defended.

"Yeah well, there is a drinking age in Pennsylvania!" he screamed and leapt towards me.

I wonder if anyone outside heard screaming that sounded like it was coming from a little girl. He kicked the snot out of me for that one. I never saw my dad drink. He got his temper all on his own, drunk on God.

Anyway, that's where I developed my love for building, Quick Builds. Having those skills was something to be proud of.

*

"Hey, that's cool. I love woodworking too. You should see my garage," Tony responded.

I snapped out of my daydream and smiled at Tony.

"Yeah, that would be cool…" I told him.

WORLDLY

Everyone was startled by the front door being thrust open. My dad charged into the house. Tony got up with a raised fist.

"Dad!" I shouted in surprise.

Tony lowered his fist and looked confused.

"Dad, I-I'm just having dinner!" I cried.

"Are they worldly, Jason?" he spouted rhetorically. "Let's go!"

My dad went to grab my hair but stopped as Tony moved toward him.

"Don't you fuckin'…" Tony started.

My dad didn't touch me, yet.

"*Move* Jason!" my father shouted.

Michelle started balling her eyes out. The whole family looked paralyzed in shock. Except for Tony, who looked like he wanted to kill my dad.

Townsend

"Jason! Don't go!" Michelle cried.

"A worldly girlfriend, huh? Nice," my Dad growled further. He was pissed.

I stared at my father a moment and squared up with him. For a split second I considered standing up to him, but then what? This family had just met me. I had not exactly made a great impression thus far, I was sure. My father seethed, he was ready for a fight. I backed down and walked past my father to the stairs. My father kicked me down them. No big deal, there were only about six stairs, I got right back up of the tile foyer. I heard Tony shout again.

Once outside, I had another problem. I walked right past my turd-brown Jetta. I pretended it was not mine and headed for our family car. I looked up and saw the Rossi kids peering out of their windows. Tony and Beverly stood on their front porch.

"No boy, I've known you bought that damn car for a while, now. Drive it home. I don't want you in my car," my father said.

WORLDLY

"You've been following me, Dad? I asked.

My dad ignored me and turned to the Rossi's.

"Now, I'm sorry, but Jason well knows that we do not associate with people outside of our faith. He should have told you," my father called to them.

My father waited for me to get in my car, glaring at me. As I drove away my dad followed behind me, tailgating me out of the neighborhood. I caught a glimpse of Beverly hugging Tony, and Michelle in the window crying.

I'm sure you can guess what happened when I got the car home. I took a good beating for that stunt. My father voluntarily revoked my driver's license and the car sat unused for a week or so while he thought about what to do with it. I was instructed to quit my job. I wasn't trusted to go to work anymore with the worldly. It was tense being in that house during the week that followed. Actually, it was downright miserable; you have more privacy in prison. Eventually, I got a break when my father was called to an "emergency Elder's meeting". My mother was sick and asleep. So, I took the spare Volkswagen key I'd made at the hardware store and took off.

Townsend

It would be another several years before I would own a cell phone, so things had to be done the hard way.

***

I busted in to Ace Hardware, scaring the shit out of Meredith.

"Where have you been?" she scolded, ignoring the customer in front of her.

"Where's Dave?" I shouted, ignoring her question.

"He's in the manager's office. Hey come here!"

I darted to the back of the store. I flung open the door to the manager's office and barreled in. Dave simultaneously tried to pull up his pants and hide the pornography on his monitor by hugging it. His pants fell to the ground.

"What the fuck!" Dave snarled over his shoulder.

Grossed out I looked up at the ceiling to address him.

"Sorry. Hey look. I've been having a real problem at home. I don't want to quit. I...love it...here," I explained.

Half an hour later Meredith and Dave joined me in the parking lot. We gathered around my Jetta.

"Wow. That's some crazy shit man. Is that where you got that shiner?" Dave asked.

"Uh huh."

"Aright, well your job is safe and look, if you need a place to stay... I live above the Sports Shop on Willow Street Road," Dave offered.

"Thanks man. I appreciate that." I said. "I might have to take you up on it."

"Yeah, I can ask my parents, maybe you can stay with us too. Like, on weekends," Meredith offered.

There was an awkward pause as my mind splashed around in the gutter.

Townsend

"Uh, yeah. Ok, I have to go now! Bye," I said rushing off.

I got in the turd-mobile and drove away. Meredith and Dave stood in the parking lot, Dave put his arm around Meredith and she swatted it away.

The next stop was the Rossi's. Tony answered the door. I asked if I could come in. Tony looked around for a moment and reluctantly let me in.

A brief time later the whole family sat at the dinner table. Michelle clung to my arm like I was dying of cancer.

"Look, Jason. I don't know what to say. It's probably wrong of me, but... you've got to get out of there. Can you stay with anyone?" Beverley asked.

I thought a moment and answered, "Yeah this guy at work said I could stay there."

Beverly said she'd like to meet him.

WORLDLY

"Look, if you want to get out, we'll support you 100 percent. But, you know, you're a minor. Your parents are legally responsible for you," Tony reasoned.

"I know, and I don't care. I've gone to church three days a week my whole life. There is not a day of the week that I am not required to do anything for the church in place of schooling. I'm not allowed to disagree with anything or think for myself. I've knocked on so many doors that I felt like I was going to be sick just knocking on yours. I can't knock on one more door. I can't go to college, I can't have a girlfriend, I can't *have friends*. I have no freedom. I hate every moment in that house. I don't care if I have to live on the *street*," I explained.

"Come here if there is a problem, OK?" Beverly said in a monotone but comforting voice.

I felt like everything was going to be OK. Like my future had just opened ahead of me. I nodded to Beverly and left with Michelle.

Michelle and I slowly strolled to my car. She still clung to my arm.

Townsend

"I'm worried about you," Michelle whispered.

I turned to her and held her tight in my arms.

"Gotta' try, right?" I said, "I can do it, don't you worry. I can do anything."

Michelle wrapped her arms tighter around my torso. I pulled away to leave and looked into her eyes. I had never seen a look from someone so concerned about me. I got lost in her eyes for a moment, then leaned in and kissed her. She kissed back with more passion. I put my chin on her shoulder and hugged her tight again.

"That was my first kiss."

"Me too," she responded.

I felt like I had a different kind of home, in her heart. I felt like I had a purpose and I wasn't alone anymore. I was finally going with the tide instead of swimming against it. I had a girl, a real girl, not a Spice Girl or a model from the lingerie section of a JC Penney catalog, and she cared about me in return.

WORLDLY

***

Once home I madly crammed my belongings in to a duffle bag. It filled up too quickly. I looked around, found my backpack, and in a furious rush I tried stuffing socks and underwear in between my school books. That filled up quickly.

This was Life Applicable Lesson No.1. This is just one of many times I experienced the fact that the things you own end up owning you, it is not just a movie quote. I sifted through my entire life trying to decide what memories to bring with me and what memories to leave behind. I had thirty minutes to pack my entire life in to a nylon bag. It was too small, so I ended up packing my life in to a forty-two-gallon garbage bag. Appropriate. I may have benefited from patience and quietly waited until the middle of the night, but my mind was made up. Every minute that would slowly tick by would have been excruciating… patience was never my forte. You only live once, better not to fart around.

I struggled to drag my trash bag of belongings out of the house. The problem was I had to pass the living room on the way out, where my dad was watching TV. I quietly tip-toed by, hoping to sneak myself and my bags past the couch unnoticed. The TV went mute.

"What do you think you're doing?" my father asked alarmed.

My heart dropped.

"*Leaving*," I answered, hearing the emotion break right through my voice.

I heard the remote control fall to the floor.

My dad began jogging towards me. I ran out the front door and squeezed the trash bag through. I shoved the storm door closed with the bag, trying to close it and consequently slow my father down. I had parked my car in the woods again, fearing my dad was planning on sabotage. I dropped my trash bag of belongings and squared off with my father for the last time. I took a step towards him and he stopped with a dumb look on his face.

"You're not leaving," my dad said. There was a little less demand in his tone, replaced with desperation.

WORLDLY

"Yea. I *am*. I'm tired of this shit!" I screamed, emotion pouring out like air from a burst balloon. "You can't beat the fear of God in to your kids! You're only breeding hatred for a world you know nothing about. Ignorance isn't bliss… it's just fucking ignorance! The only thing you've taught me to avoid…is you."

I saw the last bit of my father's patience disappear.

"I fucking hate you!" I screamed.

I truly regret that; I did not think it would be one of the last things I said to my father. My father ran over to the front yard, picked up a rock and threw it at me. I ducked as it whizzed past my head.

"Fuck you!" I yelled.

This was the first time I ever cursed at the people who brought me in to this world. I really dove in the deep end, but like I said before- I had to do everything 'balls to the wall'. I started to jog down our long driveway. A stone whizzed past me. The driveway went on forever. I turned to look back at the house and saw Louise, my little sister, looking out her bedroom window. Another stone landed nearby. I stopped in

Townsend

my tracks and stared back for a moment in complete devastation. In all the chaos I had forgotten about Louise. Tears rolled down her face, a hand on the window. I heard the family car start and realized it was time to run. The car peeled out and I hauled ass down the driveway. I felt my dad's car approaching from behind, a few feet from hitting me. I threw my trash bag onto his windshield and he swerved into a sycamore tree. I dove into the woods and continued with nothing but my backpack of school books, my father calling my name from the wrecked car.

For the last time I rolled my car out from its hiding place in the woods. As I pushed it on to River Road I could still hear my dad calling for me. My sister said my dad cried that night. I had never seen him cry. He also expressed deep regret for not home-schooling us.

That was the end of... me. I was never that Jason again. It was the end of stability. It was the end of believing I knew the answers about God and the world, but it was the beginning of me asking questions and learning about the world as honestly as possible. I was about to learn about the world I was sheltered from. My rampant curiosity was now free to be appeased and I had no idea where that would take me or how hard my lessons would be to learn. It is true that I wanted sex education and my hormones gave me the power to run, but I also wanted to learn from the entire library of life, not just the Jehovah's Witness section. Once I got the taste of running though, it never stopped.

Townsend

CHAPTER FIVE

<u>Homeless</u>

I had no choice. I had nowhere else to go. At sixteen years old I stood in front of Dave's shitty apartment, not wanting to knock. I stood broken, disheveled, empty-handed and empty-headed but immensely optimistic. I barely knocked on the door and it swung open. There Dave stood shirtless and sloppy, drunk as a skunk. I could now see Dave was a hoarder. This made me a bit itchy as I was brought up under the scripture- *cleanliness is next to godliness.* Dave must not have had a Bible; although I did try to give him one once.

"OOOHHHHH! Shit man! You really did it, huh?! You got balls bro! Come on in! Me pasta is Sue's pasta, man. Where's your stuff?" Dave greeted enthusiastically.

WORLDLY

Dave stumbled backwards trying to let me in. His eyes were as wide as golf balls and he blinked, which took him a noticeable amount of effort. I entered his apartment, grateful to have a place to go, but shocked at the state of it. I do not think he got many visitors.

"Sorry man, I forgot to tell you... I'm a fuckin' slob bro. Ha!"

"It looks like this is where they empty dumpsters," I half joked. It really did though.

"Well. Shit, pretty much. I'm always ass-up in that dumpster grabbing shit from the card shop downstairs. It's like a hobby. Want a beer man?"

"Naw, buddy. I'm OK. Thanks though," I responded. I was under the impression a solitary beer would cause me to helicopter-puke all over his apartment. Although I doubt Dave would have even cared.

"You sure? You look like you could use one..." Dave pried.

"I'm seventeen, man," I answered.

Townsend

Yes, I lied. I thought if he knew how young I really was I'd be too much of a liability. Dave looked shocked, which added to that worry.

"Uh…. *And*?" Dave continued the pressure.

Dave slumped down on his couch and turned his attention to a thirty-inch TV he kept about two feet from his face, sitting on top of a coffee table littered with garbage and drug paraphernalia. At the time I had no idea what any of the drug stuff was. I sat beside him on the couch and opened my Trapper Keeper to do my homework. Dave looked over when he heard the Velcro sound.

"What a loser."

He scoffed and slumped deeper in to his couch, spilling beer on himself. I looked down at my homework and closed my eyes, thoroughly exhausted.

What I would estimate to be about thirty minutes later I woke to being punched in the face.

"Put it back man! Put it back!" Dave shouted, irrationally irate.

I put my hands up to deflect his blows. He tried repeatedly to strike me in the face, but I swatted most of his jabs away.

"Put *what* back man?" I shouted in confusion.

"You fuckin' took it! I know you did! You little fuckin' turd! You think you're better than me?" He shouted in complete craze.

"Dude! I've been asleep since I got here! What the *fuck*?" I shouted, now irate myself.

Dave retreated to his side of the couch and sat down in a ball. He just rocked back and forth. I thought he was about to start sucking his thumb. I just stared at him in disbelief. What a way to wake up. This was not going well.

"Sorry. Sorry. I t-took some acid just before you got here. Sorry. Sorry," Dave apologized sheepishly.

I continued to stare at him in disbelief.

"You took acid?"

136

Townsend

"Yeah."

"Alone?"

***

A couple months later I really was seventeen and I could be found at pretty much any point of the day at Penn Manor High School. That was because I lived there. After the brief experience as Dave's roommate, I decided I was safer living in the Jetta, although I told the Rossi's I was still living at Dave's. One morning I crawled out of the trusty old turd mobile shirtless and with disheveled hair. I opened the Jetta's trunk and applied my deodorant. I greeted a couple walking past and staring as I grabbed a relatively fresh T-shirt from the spare tire well (it was empty because the spare tire was on the car). I fetched my backpack from the back seat, closed the trunk and locked the car. In to school I went.

It was like any other autumn day. I went inside and checked in at my locker- which was pretty much my storage unit. I grabbed a banana from the cafeteria and said hello to a friend or two (which I had considerably more of now). I was the only kid in high school who successfully ran away from home and that seemed to give me some street cred. My parents didn't really try to get me to come home. There was a little back and forth for a few weeks but after my worldly aspirations were apparent, I was written off like a bad investment. After my morning routine I ended in home room. I slumped in to my seat next to Gabe, still tired from the night before. It was September and getting a bit cold which affected my sleep. He looked over at me.

"So, what are you going to do for break? Do you want to stay at my house?" Gabe asked.

"I can't. I'm going to New York to visit Michelle's grandparents," I answered.

"Yea. I bet it's a lot different than here... I can ask my parents if you can stay at my house, dude. I feel horrible that you're sleeping in your car."

Townsend

"Ah, naw Gabe. Thanks though. It's too close to my parents. They know the car. I feel safe here in the parking lot with the security guard."

Our fifty-year-old eccentric teacher, Mr. Stucky, frantically burst in to the room and turned on the TV.

"Kids! Listen up! Front of the room! Front of the room!" he screamed so loud it scared me and I jumped in my seat and farted a little.

Mr. Stucky frantically smashed buttons on the remote trying to change the channel from the morning announcements. In his other hand he simultaneously smashed buttons on a Nokia cell phone. He screwed up the multitasking and had to lower the Nokia phone momentarily. He eventually got the remote to work and found live news. The North Tower of the World Trade Center in New York City showed smoke bleeding out of its side.

"…the fuck is that?" Gabe asked.

"I don't know…" I trailed off leaning in to see.

WORLDLY

My first thought was that some rich Hamptons dummy accidently flew his Cessna into the building, maybe trying to impress a girl. Mr. Stucky paced back and forth tugging at his hair and fumbling with his brick of a cell phone.

"Kids. You *have* to pay attention. We are so close to Three Mile Island..." Mr. Stucky warned.

The news channel broadcasted a banner: "World Trade Center, New York City".

We watched intently, completely confused. Some kids were terrified but that was not the general reaction. We thought it was a joke, that it was not genuine. We quietly focused on the TV.

"This is three hours away kids," Mr. Stucky said. "Two hours, closer if you were in a pla..."

Mr. Stucky paced like a nervous chicken. The television erupted as an object smashed in to the second tower. Mr. Stucky jumped straight up in the air and yelped out a scream that sounded female.

Townsend

"FUCK! We're all going to fucking die! *Go*! Go home! Go to your families! If you drove get the *fuck out*!" he ordered.

Mr. Stucky threw his phone to the ground. He immediately whimpered and dove after it. He got up and fetched his keys and flew the room in a panic, leaving his jacket and bag behind. I turned to Gabe and just stared. No words formed from my mouth or brain, just a squeak.

"His wife works at the Trade Center. He was just telling me about it... like a week ago. They were having problems..." Gabe said in disbelief.

Gabe and I didn't have cell phones yet. We were so confused. This was a time when we felt we were young and untouchable. I think the whole country did. The United States may have been alone in that feeling. A big hand reached out across an ocean and slapped the whole country in the face. That morning we weren't sure what was even happening. Terrorism was a word that was never real to me before. I had so many other things going on at the time. I looked back at the television one more time to see a zoomed replay of an airplane hitting the South Tower.

"Let's go, dude." Gabe ordered.

WORLDLY

***

I sat quietly in the back of the Rossi family van next to Michelle. Michelle had her head on my shoulder and rubbed my leg with her small left hand. Tony, her father, eyeballed me through the rearview mirror. It was a bit nerve-racking and I made sure to make excuses (like stretching) to make my hands visible to him. Michelle and I felt bad for feeling this way but honestly- we were excited as hell. We were on our first road trip! It was my first trip to New York. I mean, it was a terrible occasion for it, but regardless, a part of me was still excited. I had a disposable camera ready for pictures. I knew it wasn't the best occasion but maybe I could snap a few on the sly considering the subject was rare. Since I was a little boy I loved two things, taking pictures and writing stories. I liked dreaming of worlds different than my own. This seemed like an opportunity, but it also felt wrong to feel that way.

The Rossi's were the only ones in their family to leave New York, so 9/11 hit them hard. While most people were

Townsend

fleeing New York, we packed up and headed straight for it. A couple of hours after leaving Lancaster the family van screeched to a halt in Lower Manhattan. It was less than a week after the attack that we went to see it for ourselves.

I remember taking my first steps onto New York concrete. Exiting a vehicle for the first time and stepping out onto the sidewalks of New York City is like hearing a solitary note from a quiet violin followed by a hundred-piece orchestra thundering in. Sure, it is impressive to any first-timer to view through a car window, but stepping out onto the sidewalk is sensory overload, especially to a boy from quiet Amish country.

My first experience with something terrible happening in the world was during the aftermath of the 9/11 terror attacks. Upon first sight, nothing registered, I absolutely did not know what to think. It was like being in a real-life nightmare that completely overwhelms the conscious mind. I looked to Tony and Beverly for cues, but they were utterly devastated also. In their faces I saw the destruction of critical and beloved memories, a place that made up a part of their identity in ruins. It was as if someone opened their brains and vandalized their reminiscence. Have you ever seen the movie *Dante's Peak*?

WORLDLY

There is a scene where an entire town is covered in ash from a volcano beginning to erupt. To me, that's what lower Manhattan looked like, except this town was packed with 1.5 million people.

In somber silence the younger part of the group (Michelle, her brother Tim, and I) trailed behind Tony and Beverly as they walked like zombies towards Greenwich Street. I casually tried to sneak opportunities to look up and marvel at the size of the buildings left standing, but it seemed inappropriate. As we neared the site however, I kept my eyes down as I was experiencing the most wretched, dismal and devastating thing I ever hope to see. Seeing physical brick and mortar destruction on that scale is jarring, and it absolutely leaves an impression. However, it does not remotely compare to the agony I witnessed all over the sidewalks bordering Ground Zero.

The real damage of the attacks surrounded the physical wreckage. The buildings were gone, and those who died had passed on. What haunts me still were the families- hundreds of people left behind who camped on those sidewalks. Hundreds of people, all in the worst moments of their lives, had left their comfortable homes to camp on the streets of

144

Townsend

New York City. There they waited to hear the FDNY call their loved one's name and let them know what they had recovered. The city had constructed an eight-foot chain-link fence, covered in vinyl that bordered the entirety of Ground Zero. These family members and friends, as if to be as close as physically possible, made their camp along that fencing. Marriage photos, family portraits, flowers and wreaths made up individual shrines tucked into the chain link above their camps. Tributes to the victim, the person they had lost, hung above their heads as they waited.

As we walked along the fence, looking for a glimpse of what lay behind it, I realized I had experienced this feeling before. It was at a funeral. I'd had the feeling of wanting to make a grieving survivor feel better and yet recognizing it as a hopeless endeavor before. I had peered into eyes, seen the pain, and quickly looked away for the smallest touch of it was unbearable. It was that uncomfortable feeling you get consoling a survivor at a funeral, but I felt it for every single person I saw that day.

As we circled the site we encountered what I could best describe as the plank. The plank was the city's way of handling one of human nature's most morbid tendencies, the looky-loo. At a certain point, the grief-stricken survivors gave way to a single-file line of gawkers who waited for hours to walk the plank. The plank reached out in to and above the rubble of ground zero. A looky-loo could walk to the edge of hell and take a picture. We opted out of the plank experience and decided instead to head to the Rossi grandparents, on Long Island. I threw the unused disposable camera in a New York City trash can.

Townsend

CHAPTER SIX

Yo-Yo

I laughed as my teeth crunched in to fried chicken leg. I sat with the Rossi's at their kitchen table eating dinner. Beverly had an envelope next to her plate. She had been nervously tapping it with her fingernail. I thought maybe it was a bill that she wanted to discuss with Tony or some other serious thing. Maybe we were about to get scolded over the electric bill.

The Rossi's had found out that my living conditions were not exactly ideal and had taken me in. I spent the rest of my senior year of high school living with my girlfriend's family. It sounded cool, and it was, but it also led to a lot of embarrassing moments like getting caught by Michelle's grandmother with a boob in my mouth. What kind of family would let their daughter's boyfriend move in? The best one I have ever come across in life to-date, that's who. This family remains my perfect picture of what a healthy family should be. I had my own room, which was also the office, located on a squeaky floor right next to the Rossi parental units. It was situated on the opposite floor of the opposite side of the house as Michelle. I could not have been physically farther away and still inside their house. The parents were very diligent about keeping us from being alone together, which made the pursuit all that much more fun.

Beverly finally had enough and dropped her fork, it clanked off her plate.

"Sorry Tony, I can't frickin' wait any longer!" she said, turning to me and holding the envelope, which I could now clearly see had my name on it.

I was thoroughly confused; my heart jumped a bit. I didn't get mail. I wouldn't even know where to have it sent.

"Bev!" Tony shouted in mild protest.

"Jason, I have news for you," Beverly said, teeming with excitement.

Townsend

"Yeah?" I asked excitedly. "What it is?"

"You got in to Lancaster Tech!" she shouted proudly.

I was happy, don't get me wrong, but I have been more excited in my life. I was raised my whole life to understand college as a frivolous excess. Going to college brought up problems that I had no idea how to solve. I was going to have to work full-time to even afford it and I did not know where I would live.

"Oh… great!" I mumbled through a mouthful of chicken.

"*Free*," Beverly stated.

I was confused.

"Huh?"

"*Free* Jason…they gave... you won the full ride! I... I wrote them a letter," Beverly said proudly but quietly, as if she was worried she did something wrong.

"You got me a full scholarship to college?" I asked in utter disbelief. I wanted to cry.

WORLDLY

"*You did.* I just told them about you, that's all. I sent a letter in with your application. I just said what a good boy you are and how you got set behind because of your parent's, yadda, yadda, yadda."

I sobbed as I ran over and hugged Beverly in her chair. Everyone congratulated me, Michelle was a little quieter than everyone else. I felt blank.

Even though I wanted to be a regular kid, it was so hard to do. I still felt bad going against my father's wishes. I got a full ride and I didn't even really feel excited. I just felt, sinful. On the other hand, I had really liked New York.

***

On graduation night I received my diploma wearing and ear-to-ear grin. Michelle's grandparents came to see me graduate. They also came to take me to New York for the summer. The only problem was; Michelle didn't know that detail. Everyone had noticed a change in her behavior. She started to become very clingy, all she thought about was me.

Townsend

If I got up for a glass of water, she wanted to know where I was going.

The other distraction of the night was the fact that my parents had shown up. I had not spoken to them in some time, so I guess they came as a last-ditch effort to see if I was planning on coming back and joining God's workforce. It was a happy night and everyone in the building was smiling, so it was as good of a time as any to see them. I excitedly chattered to my father and mother about my scholarship to college. I recognized their pretend pleasure in the news; it was not Bethel. I turned to see the Rossi's waiting for me down the hall, watching my interaction with my parents nervously. I told my parents to take care, and I did not see them again.

***

Yet again I practiced a skill that would follow me for many years to come. I hurriedly packed my bags, I had little time. I marveled, and regretted, how many things I had come to acquire in a little over a year. I stopped in my tracks as I heard a soft tapping at the door.

"Babe? Are you OK?" Michelle quietly asked from the other side of the locked door.

I froze, locked up… no clue what to say next. Michelle needed a break to just be a teenager. I wanted to see New York for the summer. Her grandparents were ready to leave and take me with them. For some reason the adults thought it would be an acceptable idea to go to Kmart while I packed. They left Michelle home with me while I was secretly preparing to leave for New York.

"Um, yea babe. I'm… just going to stay with your grandparents for the summer," I said cautiously.

Not smart.

"*What?* Babe, no! Open the door!" she screamed.

She began to pound on the door.

"You and I were going to have a great summer together! They're *my* grandparents! Not yours!"

Townsend

She continued pounding on the door.

"No Michelle, it's OK. I'll be back. You just need to have some time just for yourself, ya' know?"

The Rossi's were the kindest people I had ever known, but it was too much for Michelle. She was two years younger than me, living with me at an age where every month matters. It just wasn't healthy for a fifteen/sixteen-year-old to live under the same roof as her boyfriend and it got to her.

The pounding on the door turned to slamming. Michelle took to running down the hallway and slamming her full ninety pounds of body weight into the bedroom door. I thought her parents would hate me if I caused a door in their house to be broken, so I leaned against the door to counter-balance the slams.

"Michelle! Stop! It'll be OK!" I shouted, trying desperately to talk her down.

The slamming stopped, and a moment of relief came over me. I stood in silence, with my weight against the door, listening. It felt too good to be true that she gave in to one sentence. I heard her footsteps approach the door again and braced for impact, but it did not happen. Instead, I heard whimpering on the other side of the door.

"I...I don't want to live without you," she sobbed.

I stared at the door trying to figure out what that meant, and what to do about it. I loved her. She was the first girl I ever loved. To think of her to this day brings a warm and fuzzy feeling to my heart... but we were so young.

"I..."

"OUCH!" Michelle whimpered.

I jumped and ripped open the door. Michelle slumped in to the room from sitting propped against the door. Blood was coming from a small horizontal slash in her left wrist. A kitchen knife lay on the ground.

"NO! FUCK! *NO!*"

I fell to the ground and held her, rocking her back and forth.

Townsend

"Look, I love you, I really do. Nothing changed there. We are just too young..." I cried.

I heard her parents and grandparents enter the front door downstairs. They chattered happily amongst themselves.

"Tony! Beverly! Quick!" I screamed. My voice cracked in tears.

Michelle hit me repeatedly and tried to crawl away, but I held on tight.

"No!" she growled to me.

The Rossi's came running up the stairs, her grandparents followed. Tony reached his daughter first and picked her up in his arms, glaring at me.

"It's time to go, Jason." he said to me sternly. He was a good dad.

I threw my bags in her grandparent's trunk and left my turd mobile parked at the Rossi's curb. As we drove down the block an ambulance rounded the corner and passed us. Her grandma sobbed in the front seat and looked longingly out of the passenger window.

I never wanted to hurt Michelle. I loved her as much as an adolescent could. I often wonder to this day what would have happened if we had been older, if we could have been high school sweethearts that stayed together and lasted forever. That is what I believed at the time, but that was not what happened. I was going to Long Island for the summer, I had just stepped foot into the real world for the first time.

***

Out of sheer boredom I went out and got a job. It was a little un-stimulating, constantly being at home with Michelle's grandparents in Long Island, day after day. I was sure they were sick of trying to entertain me. I was eighteen and in a new place, New York. Albeit only for a few months, I wanted to go out and meet people my age, real New York kids. I wanted to see how they lived and learn about a new kind of American culture that I knew nothing about. I got a

Townsend

job at Friendly's Ice Cream off Hempstead Turnpike in Levittown, New York. I either walked or Michelle's grandparents gave me a ride to work.

I scooped ice cream into a dish at the ice cream fountain. It wasn't the ideal job; I would have preferred to be a waiter. If I was a waiter, then perhaps I could meet some people and make friends. Luckily, pretty much the entire staff was around my age. People liked my Pennsylvania accent and liked to point at the 'chaw-klat' ice cream and ask me to say 'chocklat'. My feet made a sticky sound as I moved on the rubber mat, rotten ice cream stuck to the bottom of my shoes. I put the ice cream Sunday I had made on a shelf for the waitress. Gianna, a girl almost the same age, came over and placed it on her server's tray.

"Hey, do you want to come out with my friends tonight?" she asked.

I sighed and pulled at my filthy apron.

"Yeah, I sure do." I responded.

"Great you can meet some people!" she cheered.

WORLDLY

"Great! I smell like rotten ice cream, so I should be popular."

Later that night I sat on a porch swing at a house on Flamingo Lane, talking to Gianna as a party raged on inside. A group of three thuggish kids approached, all a few years older than me. I looked a little nervous and Gianna looked more than a little irritated.

"Who invited *you*?" Gianna snarled at them.

"Nice to see you too, Gianna. We're just here to chill with your sister, she's on her way. Who's your friend?" the tall one asked.

He was a big dude, six-foot-four and two-hundred-and-fifty-pounds to be exact.

"Hey Jason, I'm Matthew, this is Alec and Hubert. What's good bro?" Matt said, introducing his friends.

His vernacular confused me; these kids were significantly cooler than me by most social standards.

Townsend

"Hey man. Uh, I dunno', the p-party is pretty good," I stuttered.

"Oh, hey! You guys have something in common! Jason is an ex-J-dub like you guys." Gianna said to Matt.

"No shit?" Alec chimed in looking shocked.

I was equally as shocked. What are the chances? I partied the rest of the summer with two groups of friends. Gianna and her friends were good kids, they drank, but overall, they were the safer choice of friends. They probably had good grade point averages in high school and had bright futures ahead of them. The other group I hung out with was Matt's group, the ex-J-dubs. They were insane compared to what I had known back in Pennsylvania, but they had that one thing in common that I just could not ignore.

I did get much more of the variety I craved in New York. It was not a sea of white people. Alec was Puerto Rican. Hubert was an immigrant from Warsaw, Poland, and had a cool accent. Matt's family had emigrated from Germany at some point in recent history, but he lacked a cool accent. My curiosity was through the roof in New York.

WORLDLY

Michelle eventually came to visit in New York a couple of months later. She was very embarrassed about what had happened and was now angry with me. We tried to rekindle our relationship when she came to visit but that failed. She was not happy I had made local friends and she was still too young to join in. We grew apart quickly. I had a great summer on Long Island but before I knew it, it was over.

***

I had to go back to Pennsylvania for college. I didn't want to leave New York but I had that scholarship and my car was still parked at Michelle's house. I had just made friends in New York- my first real friends. Using my experience in Long Island, I easily got a job at the local Friendly's Ice Cream in Lancaster City. This time I scored the prestigious waiter job. No more stinky ice cream feet and there I met a girl named Larissa, another waitress.

After work one night she asked to come back with me to my dorm room. I was happy to oblige, she was attractive, and

Townsend

I had the good luck of getting a room to myself. I was supposed to have a roommate, I even knew his name, but he never actually moved in. So, I pushed both beds together and used both closets; I had a pretty sweet setup.

I snuck Larissa into my room, trying to keep her quiet. She kept getting excited at the James Bond venture to get her into the dormitory. Once in the room I locked the door, sighed and laughed in relief. I sat a plastic shopping bag down on my coffee table and pulled a bong out from under it. Larissa swiftly sat down next to me, ready to partake. We smoked a bong-load, and I pulled a forty-ounce beer from a shopping bag. I put on my favorite movie, *Half Baked*. During my entire college career, I do not think that DVD ever left the player. I cranked up the sound to my surround sound as the movie started. I took a swig from my forty, and nervously snuggled with Larissa, offering her a sip.

"How did you get a room to yourself? Larissa asked,

"My roommate came here the first day and just left. He said he was getting a house with a bunch of his friends, I guess. Fine with me!" I told her.

WORLDLY

"Yeah, you're lucky...and you can have girls over and stuff?" she asked.

"Oh, hell no, this is Bible country! No way," I replied.

"Wow, so this is like… forbidden, huh?" she asked while playfully rubbing my leg.

I smiled and kissed her. We were brutally interrupted by a sharp pounding on the door.

"Shit, shit, shit. Quick! Get in the closet… it'll be OK." I whispered.

I walked Larissa over to a closet and hid her behind clothes. The door erupted again.

"Shit!" I whispered to myself.

I composed myself and cracked the door to find Pokey, the disabled security guard. Pokey embraced the nickname. Hell, he might have come up with it himself. He was a guy in his forties missing both of his arms, yet a single finger protruded from either shoulder. The sleeves of his security guard uniform were hemmed up so that he had use of the appendages. A walkie-talkie handset was mounted within reach of one of his fingers. The first thing Pokey did at orientation was joke about his condition, trying to make all of us young bastards accept him. I thought it was unnecessary as I would have liked him anyway, he was a cool guy. He was a hardcore Christian, but a hell of a lot nicer than the off-duty cop on the same shift.

"Dang, Pokey! You scared me!" I greeted him.

Anyway, I would have picked a different nickname for Pokey. I would have picked Rooster. The guy walked around like a chicken. He would pace up and down the hallways and when he heard something suspicious he would lean over and put his ear up to door and listen (which by the way is complete horse-shit). When Pokey heard, or smelled, something he didn't like, there he'd go, pecking away. He did not have the luxury of a phalangeal knock, so he would head-butt the door instead. This, as I am sure you could imagine, makes a hell of a startling racket.

"Why do you have to head-bang the door man? I just got back from work and I'm trying to sleep," I complained.

WORLDLY

"Yeah, OK Jason. Well, I'm sorry to bother you but I heard a... *female*... voice in here," Pokey poked.

I looked back over my shoulder scanning the room for a moment, then back at Pokey.

"No female. I'm just watching a movie. Girls are in the movie. I have surround sound man, it's a really sweet system, Pokey. I guess it was a little loud. I'll turn it down. Sorry," I said trying to put a polite end to the conversation.

"Mind if I poke around?" he asked, seriously oblivious to the pun.

I gave him an irritated look for a moment before letting him in.

Pokey strolled around the dorm room. He crouched and contorted as he looked around for contraband. I almost lost it when Pokey stood right next to my forty-ounce beer, but I kept quiet. He did not notice it. He continued over to the closet. He looked at my clothes a moment... then buried his fucking face in the closet and wagged it around. This caused Larissa to bust out laughing. Pokey pulled his head out of my closet, eyes wide in excitement.

Townsend

"*Girl*!" Pokey shouted as if he had just found a Russian spy.

"*Oh*, shit." I groaned into my hands.

"Come out! Come out girl!" Pokey ordered.

I thought about how this is really going to affect my chances with Larissa. She climbed out of my closet, laughing uncontrollably. She looked at Pokey in disbelief, then at me, flabbergasted.

"What the fuck, dude?" Larissa asked, and resumed laughing.

I had been demoted to "dude". I thought I may as well give up on trying to date Larissa ever again. Pokey wrapped his finger around his walkie handset and it chirped.

"Pokey to base! Pokey to base! We've got a situation in room two-thirteen! We've got a girl!" he shouted in excitement like he had just caught a Marlin.

"You! You stay here! Don't move or go anywhere," Pokey commanded Larissa.

WORLDLY

I thought about how boring this college must be, judging by his excitement at finding a girl in my room. It was not exactly what I would consider a big fish.

Pokey finished the transmission and began rigorously walking around the room, darting his eyes and scanning for contraband. On his second pass he found the forty sitting by the coffee table. Pokey jumped straight up in to the air.

"Oh! Oh my God! *BEER!*" his voice cracked as he exclaimed and got back on his radio.

"Pokey to base! Pokey to base! We've also got underage drinking! Repeat we've got beer in two-thirteen! Call for police backup!"

That is when I lost it with Pokey. I'd had enough. I spent all night working and got lucky enough to have a girl I like want me back for only the second time in my short life. He just ruined that. Now he is going to call the *cops* because I am eighteen and quietly having a beer? I was not throwing a party. I was a college student relaxing after work with a beer and a girl. If I was not doing that in my thirties someone would ask me what was wrong with my life. I picked up the forty.

Townsend

"What... what are you doing? Put that down," Pokey ordered me.

"You said there was beer," I calmly said to him.

I opened the window to my dorm room that faced the football field. I threw the bottle into an overgrowth of bushes that bordered the field.

"What beer?" I rhetorically asked.

Pokey jumped again in excitement.

"Oh! You're in big trouble now! Obstruction of justice, buddy! That's what that is!" Pokey hollered.

"You are not a cop, Pokey. You're just trying to ruin my life," I told him.

"Oh, Jason. You really should really get into church. You're in big trouble. You keep this up you're gonna' be burnin' fella!" Pokey lectured.

A second security guard showed up, Carl, the off-duty cop. Carl more aptly resembled law enforcement. He had a

WORLDLY

short flattop haircut and a stocky build. Carl looked considerably less engaged by the situation. In fact, it looked like we had awakened him from a nap. I think Carl had fried bigger fish in his other employment. He must have really needed the money to be working this job with Pokey. I wondered if maybe he had a gambling problem, which led me to wonder if gambling was any fun.

"Carl, you watch these two, I've got to go recover the contraband. This guy just *tossed* it out the *window*. Can you believe it?" Pokey exclaimed.

"Stay." Pokey demanded of Larissa and scampered off.

"Yeah," Carl answered, still lacking enthusiasm.

Carl smirked at me and gave me a thumbs-up. He sat down on my bed and ate a piece of gum. I thought maybe he was going to finish his nap. He picked up my remote and resumed *Half Baked* instead.

"Ha! Love this movie..." Carl laughed.

Larissa and I exchanged confused looks.

Townsend

"Uh, so what's the plan, sir?" I asked.

"Police are coming," Carl muttered.

"COPS? Over a forty and a girl? Are you serious?" I cried.

"Pokey sure is," Carl responded.

Carl shrugged his shoulders. I paced nervously, thinking of the consequences.

"He's not finding that bottle. It's gone," I told Carl.

"I dunno', man. He's pretty determined."

Pokey came back quickly with the neck of the forty held in his arm socket-finger. I was exasperated. I threw my hands down and packed a backpack.

"Hey…what? What are you doing?" Pokey asked.

"Well. It looks like I'm going to need to pack my things, aren't I?" I muttered.

"No. You're going with the police. You don't need to pack."

Carl glanced at me and then back at the TV.

"Carl, you're a cop… a little help?" Pokey begged.

"I'm off duty and he's just a kid," Carl complained.

Now that I felt validated I grabbed some paperwork, my wallet and a few of my favorite items of clothing and threw it into a bag. I looked at Pokey who was now standing over Carl getting ready to harass him for help. Carl continued to ignore him. I smiled at Pokey, grabbed Larissa by the elbow and darted out the door.

We ran downstairs together, leaving as we came- in James Bond fashion. Once outside we stood by our respective cars. I threw my bags in the backseat of the trusty old turd mobile and closed the door. I saw a police car in the distance waiting at a red light, turn signal indicating to enter the school parking lot.

Townsend

"Just get in your car and go Larissa. They aren't cops. They can't hold you. You didn't do anything. I did," I tried to reason.

"I don't know...but I feel like I should wait, like it's wrong. That crazy guy said I had to stay." Larissa objected.

"Just *go*. Why get in trouble? Look, don't think about it. Just *get in* there. Those guys up there aren't cops. Those guys *there*...are," I said pointing off at the police car that was still waiting at the traffic light.

"*Please* get in your car and go, now. I'll message you on AIM later. Please. I will feel awful if you get in trouble because of this, there is no reason to."

"No, don't worry. My mom will find this fucking hilarious. Who would believe it? Where are you going to go? Wanna' come to my house?" She asked.

"Home. I'm going home."

That was the end of my college education. I had better places to be and better things to do. The things I was curious about and wanted to learn they did not teach in classrooms. I took off as fast as my Jetta could accelerate out of the school campus, waiting for the police car to disappear between buildings, it headed to the administration building. My adrenaline pumped so hard and I went so fast when I saw my opportunity that I ripped the exhaust off on a speed bump. The pipe connecting to the catalytic convertor fell off and caught the ground, ripping the entire system, including the muffler, off my car. I pressed on anyway and sped away from the school, although no longer inconspicuous.

My car was so loud it was almost impossible to drive, and I had very little money. So, I drove to a family member I hardly knew, my father's brother. He was a respected mechanic, but we were forbidden to know him as he had no interest in the Jehovah's Witnesses. My uncle had also gotten a divorce which basically made him despicable to my parents. If we saw him, I was told not even to smile. I never understood, he was a happy-looking, clean-cut man. His kids liked him. He had a good business. Even his ex-wife came to see him for her oil changes. We were seemingly the only people in the entire world that thought he was a bad guy. I slept in the parking lot of his shop and he tapped on my window in the morning.

Townsend

Even though I was forbidden from even saying hello to my own uncle, he helped me. He put an entirely new exhaust system on my car while I waited and charged me nothing for it. I do not know what I would have done if he hadn't helped me, and I realized that I was at a loss for having been deprived of my Uncle John.

A couple months later I could be found on stage in the Long Island punk-scene, chugging from a handle of cheap vodka, dressed in women's underwear and playing drums in a girl's punk band called Pink Paisley Sofa.

CHAPTER SEVEN

New York

I was back living in New York. Gianna's family had taken me in and I was hanging out with Matthew, Alec and Hubert almost every day. One night the four of us were all packed in to my car. I listened to a rough recording of one of our Pink Paisley Sofa songs when Matt leaned over and turned the volume down. He obviously did not think it was as great as I did, and I was rather disappointed. The turd mobile had gotten some New York upgrades. Matt helped redo the stereo system and it sounded great with two twelve-inch subwoofers in the back. When it was cranked it hit so hard that you could not swallow, and you might feel like you would throw up. It was great.

I drove the trusty old Jetta down the streets of Massapequa, New York while Alec looked for a house he

Townsend

recognized. Hubert was on the phone with his girlfriend and not at all happy to be there. Hubert played with his silver chain with a giant scorpion pendant that hung around his neck. He was nervous. Matt squinted out of the passenger window.

"Man, you guys are so fuckin' stupid," Hubert complained in his thick Polish accent.

"Yo', we're here nigga'. Relax," Alec said, also on his cell phone in the back seat.

I nervously drummed my fingers on the steering wheel. Matt finished a blunt and tossed it out of a crack in the window and onto the snow just as I rolled through a stop sign.

"Hey, man. You wanna' go to a meeting this weekend?" Matt asked slowly with bloodshot eyes.

I nodded sarcastically.

"Yeah, sure man," I responded.

"Well, calm the fuck down so we're not sitting in jail instead, alright? Stop running stop signs; we've got felonies in our pockets. It's gonna' be fine, bro. Just drive straight and obey the laws," Matt said, surprising me with his sudden sobering tact.

"OK," I replied, this time lacking sarcasm.

A white blur ran past the VW and into the headlights of the car. An overly muscled guy, who looked like he had been on steroids since birth, stood in front of the car wearing white velvet sweat pants, no shirt, and a big gold chain. He spread his arms open revealing a prominent Italian flag tattoo on his chest. This was Giovanni and he was high as fuck.

"What the fuck bitches?" he screamed, and it echoed in the street.

I looked around to see if we were attracting attention. Giovanni then let out a hyena-like yelping sound and jumped on the hood of my precious turd. Six-foot-five Matt got out and threw him like a rag doll in to the snow.

"What the fuck, Gio? Are you fucking crazy?" Matt hollered.

"Ah! No shit, *asshole*! Where's the fuckin' blow?" Giovanni yelled at the top of his lungs.

Townsend

Matt took a step towards him like he was going to knock the shit out of him.

"Shut the fuck up! Here! Way to keep a low profile, ya' dumb fuck," Matt said, starting to find it funny and laughing it off.

Giovanni and Matt went in for a handshake and slammed into each other. In that brief instant Matt slipped a sack into the back of Giovanni's sweat pants and took a wad of cash from his hand. Matt pushed Giovanni away from him and jumped into the passenger seat of my car. Giovanni had his arm elbow-deep down the back of his sweat pants, digging a bag of cocaine out of his ass cheeks.

"Go, Jason! Go!" Matt yelled as he closed the passenger door.

Giovanni jumped on all fours onto the hood of my car as I peeled away. I screamed in terror. I floored the gas pedal and then smashed the brake, sliding on a patch of snow. Giovanni flew off the hood of my car and into a snow bank piled around some trash cans. My heart stopped for a moment wondering if I had killed him. We all stared out the windshield in nervous silence at Giovanni's slumped-over body in the headlights. A few seconds later he sprang to life.

"*Woo*! Yea bitch! Good shit, B! Can't kill me baby! Can't kill a stallion!" Giovanni hollered.

I begged to differ but did not even have time to sigh in relief. I held my breath and floored the accelerator again, spinning the front wheels, this time avoiding Giovanni.

Matt hung out of the passenger window flicking him off.

"Thank you, come again, muthafucka'!" Matt yelled at Giovanni.

Needless to say, selling coke to New York Italians was a new experience for me. I looked in my rear-view mirror to see Giovanni's sister Annabelle come running out of the house and punch him straight in the jaw. We all cringed, that girl could really fucking hit. For me, it was love at first sight. The car turned down Wantagh Avenue and they disappeared from my mirrors.

"Poor Gio," Alec said.

Townsend

"Oh yeah, poor Gio," I said sarcastically.

I felt like it was fate that I met these guys. I mean, what are the chances? I'm in New York for a week or two and I make friends with a group of ex-Jehovah's Witnesses? The problem was that these guys really flew the coop. They did what was expected of them, they went off the deep end when they left the cult. They stopped selling Jesus and switched to drugs. That really wasn't in my five-year plan. Not that I even had a plan besides doing every forbidden thing I could. Hubert was doing better than the rest of us; after all he could afford that custom chain. Hubert gave us someone to look up to. He had a respectable job and a nice girlfriend that he was going to marry. We all loved her too. He was a bit older and tried to keep us out of trouble. Unfortunately, we lost our positive influence a few months later.

Hubert had called me to tell me he was coming over one day after work, and I am still waiting for him to show up. He was cut off exiting the Meadowbrook Parkway by someone who was not paying attention. He swerved onto the shoulder at high speed trying to control his bike and was decapitated by a telephone pole. One of the worst ideas I ever had was to go to the scene to verify. For years I wore a piece of his broken

WORLDLY

visor on my keychain that I had picked out from washed chunks of my friend's brain. Road crews often do a lousy job of cleaning up bodies.

For once in my life I was kind of popular, although maybe with the wrong people. I had friends, drugs, a band, my own apartment, my own car and a decent job. I was doing exactly what I had always dreamed, I was free to do whatever I wanted to do, unfortunately there wasn't much of a planned trajectory. In fact, with Hubert now gone, I was the only one with a decent job. At nineteen I found a call-center job with a major insurance company as a claims examiner. I worked the mid-shift, so I could do coke, party all night and not have to wake up early. I managed to fuck that up eventually, but I didn't care. All I cared about was having fun and doing everything I was told never to do. I had a fuck-it bucket list.

Sometimes I would do coke at my cubicle at work. I would pick a mostly unoccupied section to sit in that was dimly lit. There I would sit, tie over my shoulder, snorting fat lines off my desk. If the phones were slow and I got bored, I would stay clocked into my phone and just take off. I feel bad for whoever had the misfortune of being routed to my desk after a car accident. My pre-recorded message would go off,

Townsend

so they would think I was there. The policyholder would no doubt rattle on about how some asshole that just stopped short in front of them. They would undoubtedly rant about how they were forced to rear-end them, so it is not their fault. Meanwhile I would be at the bar slamming jaeger-bombs. They said the call *could* be monitored or recorded back then, but they rarely were. It was a risk I was willing to take, especially on second shift. I would stop in at the end of the night to clock back out… and sometimes I would have to use the bathroom anyway.

I thought I was living my life, but really, I was falling apart and doing exactly what my parents expected of me.

***

Matt, Alec and I were lying around Matt's room passing a bong in a circle. We were really depressed from Hubert's passing. Matt and Alec got matching mushroom tattoos- Hubert's favorite hallucinogen. I did not want a mushroom on my body, so I got a scorpion on my back- remembering his chain and the fact he was a proud Scorpio. Our tattoos were still scabbed. In Matt's closet, the door to his safe was half open. Matt had just pulled his weed stash out. We finished the bong and sat around in depressed silence for a moment. Matt and Alec were dressed in baggy hoodies and cargo sweatpants. I was still dressed from work in a pulled-out button-down-shirt, untied tie and slacks. I sipped a beer until Matt broke the silence.

"I gotta' make some money... make Hubert proud," Matt groaned.

"Man, I told you about that teeny-bopper MacArthur kid. Five hundred E-pills bro. He's good *tonight*. Get off your lazy azz and let's do it, bro," Alec said.

Matt was hesitant.

"What does a high school kid want with five hundred Ecstasy pills?" I asked.

"Who gives a fuck? He could be given' it to his granny to help with her depression for all I care. We're about the hustle bro. Get that money," Alec whined.

Townsend

Matt sighed, sat up and rubbed his thighs. He looked at me and I looked at Alec.

"Get that money? Get a job," I said while handing him the bong.

Alec puffed up but couldn't think of a retort. Unimpressed with Alec's threatening body language I turned to Matt.

"You wanna' roll with me?" Matt asked.

I checked the time on my old Nokia cell phone.

"Nah, I can't. I have to get back to Annabelle," I laughed and spit out smoke from a cigarette. "She's probably going to kick my ass already."

"Not again..." Matt replied with a laugh.

"Yo, what you talkin' 'bout, bro? *I'll* go with you," Alec whined.

"No way, dumbass. I'd rather go by my-damn-self," Matt responded to Alec.

WORLDLY

Matt went into his safe and opened the cracked door. He pulled out a tightly-packed Ziploc bag full of pressed Ecstasy pills. He stuffed it in one of the pockets of his baggy cargo sweatpants. He stood up straight, pulled his hood over his head and stared at Alec. Alec stared back. Matt turned back to the safe and locked the door.

"Whatever, bro'," Alec smirked.

I got up and zipped a thick hoodie over my dress clothes and put on a Yankee's beanie. Matt fetched his car keys. The three of us left the smoky bedroom and walked through the living room, past a kitchenette to the back door. Matt turned to Alec.

"You gonna' hold down the fort, brother?" Matt asked.

"Alright. I got you," Alec responded.

Matt and I looked suspiciously at Alec. We decided there was no choice but to trust him, so we slapped palms, snapped fingers and left the house.

Matt and I walked down his driveway to our cars parked on the street. Matt glanced at a Ford Crown Victoria on big

Townsend

rims parallel-parked a few cars down from the cul-de-sac. I pulled my hood up over my beanie and looked at Matt.

"You OK now, brother?" Matt asked.

"Yeah, I'm good now. Thank you," I responded.

We slapped palms, got in our respective vehicles and left, my stereo blasting *Disturbed- Down with the Sickness* on the way out.

***

Inside Matt's house Alec dead bolted the back door. He exhaled deeply and strolled back to Matt's room. He casually jiggled the safe door to find it had indeed been locked tight. He flopped down on the fake leather desk chair in front of Matt's drafting table. He used this table for cutting cocaine and a few lines were left cut out but nothing substantial. He grabbed a remote control off the bed and pointed it at the TV. A South Park episode erupted from the television.

WORLDLY

"HELL YEA!" Alec chuckled at the TV. "South Park the shit, Holmes. Fuckin' stupid-ass Kenny always dyin' and shit."

Alec sat in boredom only for a few moments before his idle hands started to feel the urge to wander. He belly-laughed at a joke coming from the television. He tried to stop laughing and stop his breathing before he snorted a little mound of coke with his bare nose. He got up and shook his head, slapped his face, and the coke took hold. Alec got into Matt's dresser, rifling around through his things. He found a loose, diamond-shaped blue pill. He proceeded to smell it before he shrugged and gulped it down the hatch. Alec pulled out a tube sock with two fingers, gagged and put it right back.

"Ya' whackin' sock, bruh? Hard as a fuckin' rock, B," Alec muttered to himself.

He opened another drawer and his eyes lit up like headlights in a dark alley as he pulled out an old revolver.

"*Hell yeah.*"

Alec spun the cylinder and posed like a cowboy. He tried to open the cylinder but had no clue how. Alec rummaged through the drawer some more looking for a box of bullets but finding none. On the top of the dresser he found a loose twenty-dollar bill and snatched it up. He tucked the revolver in the waistband of his baggy sweatpants and blew a raspberry, bored as hell. He slinked back over to the drawing table and tightly rolled the twenty-dollar bill in to a straw, returning to South Park. He snorted a bigger line of coke and this time wiped his nose in pain.

"Hell yeah!" he rejoiced, squinting his watering eyes.

A moment passed, and he pulled out the revolver to play with it some more. Just then Matt's bedroom door kicked open abruptly. Alec screamed like an eight-year-old girl and threw his hands up, sending the revolver flying. The gun hit the ceiling and landed on the bed like a brick. Three Crip thugs dressed in black and blue and wearing ski masks held shotguns at Alec's face. One of them grabbed the revolver with one hand from the bed keeping his sawed-off shotgun trained on Alec. Alec's knees went weak and he dropped to the floor and began to sob. One of the Crips approached Alec who had raised his hands in surrender and rested the middle of his double-barrel shotgun on the bridge of Alec's nose.

"Where's that fuckin' safe, Alec?"

Alec looked confused that he knew his name. The man poked Alec in the face with the gun barrel. Alec whimpered and pointed to the closet where the safe sat clearly exposed.

"Open it!" the man yelled.

"I-I I don't know the combo, dawg!" Alec whimpered.

One of the Crips pointed his shotgun at Matt's TV and blew it to smithereens. Alec covered his ears in pain. Everyone winced from the sound of the fired shot in such a small room.

"OPEN IT!" the leader yelled once more.

"*What?*" Alec screamed back, still deaf.

"The fucking combination! *Fuckin' open it!*" the leader snapped, losing his patience with Alec.

"Would you tell me?" Alec whimpered.

"What?" the leader yelled, also realizing he could not hear so well anymore.

Townsend

"Bro! If you know me, right? You know my name, so you must know something about me..." Alec started, "...if you know me would you tell me the combination to *your* safe?"

The leader scoffed, looked over his shoulder at his accomplice and shrugged.

"I can't hear shit," the accomplice complained to the leader while shaking his head.

The leader got frustrated and looked at the ceiling.

"I do *not* know it. I'm pro'blly the reason why he locked it, Holmes," Alec continued.

The leader sighed and motioned to the third Crip. They rocked the safe back and forth, but it did not budge. The leader kicked it several times. The wood floor in Matt's closet cracked and the safe pulled free from its lag bolts. The second Crip joined the third, and they both lifted the safe and carried it out of the room. The leader kept his shotgun trained on Alec as the other thugs waddled away. The safe disappeared out of the room. Alec heard the back door open and his heart sank in despair as he realized the rest of the coke had just walked out the door.

We found out later this was Kevin- one of Alec's Crip "buddies" who fronted us a pound of coke. Alec had snorted so much of it we were behind in paying, so he was really just back to repo his own coke and probably kick our asses for messing up. Alec whimpered, and refused to look at the gun or Kevin. He waited, shotgun trained steady at Alec's face. Alec's gray sweatpants suddenly had a growing wet spot on the front. It was now or never. Kevin smirked, threw the shotgun over his shoulder and kicked a Timberland boot heel into Alec's forehead.

Kevin, with his shotgun barrel over his shoulder, left Matt's room. He followed the same path his accomplices did earlier, leaving through the back door. Dazed and confused, Alec made out the sound of another door being kicked open. Kevin turned around to see Matt's dad, who was as tall as Matt but with a retired body-builder's physique. He had crazy long red hair down his back. He stood shirtless and holding a samurai sword over his head. Kevin's eyes filled the holes in his ski mask.

Townsend

"Oh, shit! What the fuck nigga'?" Kevin screamed.

Kevin was not really there to kill anyone, we brought the guy video games and pizza for God's sake, but he was not expecting Matt's dad. He was not about to shoot a fifty-year-old white guy in his own home, knowing in the brief second that he had to consider it, the police would never stop looking for him if he did. Matt's dis-fellowshipped father screamed some awful rebel yell and charged Kevin with the sword. Kevin darted out of the house and the sound of tires screeching away quickly followed.

***

I had just left Alec at Matt's house and was on the way home. I heard Annabelle's voice ringing in my ears over the sound of crunching metal and glass.

"Wear your seatbelt or you'll end up going through the windshield!" the voice rang in my head.

WORLDLY

I was sprawled out on the hood of the turd mobile, her broken glass in my clothes. I wiped my face looking for blood but found none. Luckily for me it was chilly, and I had my thick hoodie with the hood pulled up over a beanie. The turd mobile's skid marks were a-hundred-and-forty-feet long and led to where I smashed into two parked cars- in a quiet neighborhood in Seaford, New York. I was not wearing my seatbelt and the impact ejected me through the windshield, the steering wheel acting as a pivot point. This is more apt to happen if you prefer the leaned-back position for your driver's seat. It leaves much more room for your body to travel in an impact and allows for more lift.

I thought about what led me to this point. At twenty-years-old I had asked my short-time girlfriend Annabelle to move in with me. She had a bit of a fiery temper and when we would fight I would go for a drive. That night, I was so upset I thought it a brilliant idea to down half a bottle of wine, a thirty-two ounce can of eleven-percent beer, and a couple ounces of Jägermeister on the way to Matt's house to talk it out. It is estimated that I left his twenty-five miles-per-hour limit backstreet doing sixty-five miles-per-hour and impacted around fifty. I remember head-banging to *Down with The Sickness* like an angry, feral idiot before losing control. I rear-

Townsend

ended a parked SUV, pushed it into another vehicle and pushed both into the middle of the street.

I wondered what the insurance company I worked for would say as I lifted my head and rolled over.

"Oh, he's alive," I heard a voice say dryly nearby.

I looked over to see a that a crowd had gathered around the accident scene.

"Are you drunk?" a pedestrian asked me.

I thought of my training at work, taking first reports of accidents. I would be written up if my first question to them was anything other than regarding their well-being.

"Am I drunk? How about "are you OK"? Ever think of that? Of course, I'm drunk you fuck," I growled at the pedestrian.

The pedestrian scoffed as I rolled off my crinkled fender and onto my feet. The crowd took a step back. I brushed the remaining glass off my clothes, pushed through the crowd and stepped away.

WORLDLY

"Hey! Where are you going?" I heard the same person ask.

I turned around to see a woman looking through my passenger window and pointing, probably at one of the empty bottles I had left on the seat.

"Hey! Your mother's house!" I yelled back and started to run.

I heard the crowd stir in confusion as I ran faster with every step. I did not want to lose my job. I had trouble thinking. I promised if I could just get out of this I would never take it for granted again. My parents would expect me to end up in jail, a product of 'the world'.

"It figures, he left the Truth. He is lost," they would reason to each other, feeling reassured and justified for writing me off.

I cut through several back yards, trying to organize a plan in my head. Ouch, my head hurt like hell. I thought about running back to Matt's house. I was running in the opposite direction of Matt's; I did not know exactly where I was going. I hid in a bush in a backyard to think. *I'll get back on the*

Townsend

highway and run home. It's only like eight miles. I'll get in bed and pretend I was asleep. The car must have been stolen- I thought to myself. Brilliant plan. I continued running through the backyards and towards where I knew an entrance to the Seaford/Oyster Bay Parkway to be.

I popped out of the backyards and onto the sidewalk just as a police car was passing, entering the neighborhood. It immediately screeched to a halt. I ran faster in the opposite direction. I heard a car door slam and footsteps running behind me.

"Stop! Nassau P.D.!" the police officer yelled.

I ran harder but was tired and possibly concussed. The police officer caught up quickly and I felt him grab for my arm. I spun around and slapped at him like a six-year-old on a playground, knocking off his hat. This gave me a burst of adrenaline, I ran harder for the salvation of the Seaford/Oyster Bay Parkway, where I surely could not be apprehended. My plan could still work. About two seconds later I was tackled by the legs and my chin slammed into the concrete, I bit my tongue. The police officer rolled me over; I was dazed and not sure if I would stay conscious.

WORLDLY

Boof. Boof.

Two heavy punches landed on my cheeks, the impacts sounding like someone diving in a pool when you are already under water. I started to cry.

"You just assaulted a police officer, kid. Dumb move!" the cop yelled, out of breath and severely irritated.

"Oh, no! I'm sorry!" I sobbed and whaled like a three-year-old. I was getting younger by the minute.

***

About an hour later my head swelled and pulsed as I lay on a wooden slab in a holding cell in Nassau County Jail. I woke to a jailor rapping on the cell bars.

"Hey! Wake up, your lawyer is here," the jailer grunted.

Townsend

I jutted up so fast the blood rushed back to my head and I thought my eyes would pop out. I had never met a real lawyer before, I thought of Don Knotts for some reason.

A round man in a cheap suit, a Disney tie and a kippah stood at my cell with a warm smile. He looked nothing like Don Knotts, he looked more like William Shatner in his 60's. I thought how nice something as simple as receiving a smile can feel after a night like that; when you have screwed up so bad that everyone hates you just for existing.

"Jason?" he said.

I smiled and stuck my hand through the bars. He looked reluctant to shake my hand at first but gave in after a moment and shook it anyway.

"Thank you so much for coming to help," I said with overwhelmingly earnest gratitude.

"Yeah, yeah, no problem, Annabelle called me. You gotta' nice girl there. Looks like you might get lucky with this stunt, but we'll have to see what happens."

I tightened my grip on the cell bars, worried.

WORLDLY

"Look. I talked with your girlfriend. She is calling your job to let them know you are sick with laryngitis and can't speak therefore you will be out of work. Considering the fact that you are a claims adjuster for car accidents, a felony DUI is not going to sit very well. However, your employment may help your case in here, considering you have no priors and a decent job," David encouraged.

"You think I'll lose it? My job?" I whined through the bars.

"Not if I can help it. They don't need to know this ever happened. A DUI will be something they will find and ultimately terminate you for upon your yearly review. So... let's hope I can knock this puppy down to somethin' that won't cost you your fuckin' job."

"OK."

"It's the weekend. Sit tight. You'll be arraigned on Monday morning, we'll post your bail and then we will talk," David continued.

"Monday? Dang. OK," I whined some more.

Townsend

"'Dang' is right. Monday. You'll have about thirty hours or so to contemplate what got you in to this mess... I don't get it. You look good on paper. No priors, so I think I can work with it, but you're messing up, kid. You gotta' take care of that girl of yours. You've been hanging with the wrong crowd," David lectured.

I thought about the first time I saw Annabelle, in my rearview mirror punching her brother Giovanni in the jaw. She was a lover in her own way. I pictured how thick she must have laid it on for this guy, and it sure worked. She had street smarts I could not have in a hundred years.

"Yeah..." I sighed under my breath.

"By the way, your buddy Matt... is in the cell block over," David said.

"*Huh?*"

"Yeah, I'll tell him you said hi," he responded kind of tauntingly.

My mind raced for answers but came up with nothing but a splitting headache.

"Matt Bloom?" I asked for clarity.

"Yep. Got caught selling five-hundred E pills to the DEA," he stated gruffly.

I looked at him, stunned. A string of drool may have dropped from my mouth.

"Anyway, you're not going be seeing Matt for a long time. That many pills are considered Attempted Manslaughter. I'd suggest a change, Jason. You seem like a good kid. Let me stress this to you, this is official advice, as your lawyer. You're payin' for it so you listenin'...? Do *not* see Matt Bloom while he's out on bail. His mom is putting their fucking house up against my advice. Don't... *fucking...* do it," David sternly advised.

I looked at my feet and felt like crying again. I was in a nightmare that I had tailor made. It was not all Matt's fault. I had felt grateful just to have a friend like Matt, and for his taking me in as part of their group. That had never really happened to me before. We had a similar upbringing and could relate, and that was hard to find. I was more socially acceptable by their association. Alec was an Elder's kid too,

Townsend

but they had all left a long time ago, able to support each other through it.

I got lucky with that stunt. I was one month away from turning twenty-one. The police officer dropped the assault charge because I was a dumb little shit with no record, and I had a respectable job that catered to government employees. I walked away with an impaired driving charge, five years suspended driver's license, a six-thousand-dollar attorney fee and a six-thousand-dollar bill from the state of New York. Impaired driving- that's like if you forget to wear your fucking glasses when you drive.

***

I took a cab home, but things were not the same. Everything was beginning to pile up. This last experience had burst my bubble- I, in fact, was not untouchable. Terrible things could certainly happen if you take the wrong chances. Unhappiness was welling up inside me and quickly becoming an uncontrollable monster. My search for independence was leaving me unsatisfied. I even had recently started playing Russian roulette on the regular, in the form of cheating on Annabelle. The lawyer's words were ringing in my ears: "*You gotta' take care of that girl*".

WORLDLY

I thought back on one early morning I was asleep in bed next to Annabelle. It was about four months prior to the accident. I had a basement apartment, so it is especially dark in there with the shades drawn. I kept my bed in the corner of the room. Annabelle was face-down and tucked against the wall, quietly sucking on her spit.

I slept with my feet on Anna's. I felt safer being asleep if I knew where she was exactly. Even in my sleep it was a surprise to feel a hand on my face. I woke abruptly to the back of female fingers, the interphalangeal joints, stroking my cheek. My eyes shot wide open.

"Morning Pumpkin,." a voice whispered softly.

I recognized the voice as belonging to Liz, a punk groupie I had met while playing drums years before. Even when I was single I avoided her advances for a long time, scared of her aggressiveness. When the empty hole in me decided to cheat, I called Liz, knowing it was a sure thing. It may have been a sure thing, but she was equally terrifying *all* the time, as Annabelle could be *some* of the time.

Townsend

I squinted in the dark, wondering if this was some brutal nightmare I had just concocted to torture myself. I made out Liz's silhouette, frizzy hair poking out from under a skull-and-bones patched snow cap. I recognized her unique smell of Camel cigarettes and Flowerbomb perfume. Nope, this was too real to be anything but.

"What *the fuck*?" I growled in low-whisper.

My subconscious, in full flight instinct mode, had automatically pre-calculated the most optimal escape route. I jumped up and darted out of the bedroom with about three swift motions. I rushed past Liz and ran into the living room, the kitchen, and -well fuck it- straight outside to the street.

I stood bent over hyperventilating on my freezing sidewalk at seven-forty-five in the morning, trying to catch my breath. I turned and faced my apartment, waiting nervously for the mushroom cloud. There was no explosion and Liz happily trotted outside after me as if nothing were wrong.

"What's wrong you *silly*? It's cold out here," she cheered, her voice sounding as if it were two in the afternoon.

I gave her a confused look but said nothing. I just examined her and wondered if she really had completely missed noticing the other girl in my bed. I tested her eyes again, looking for any masked fury. Nope, nothing but pure, unadulterated giddiness.

"Uh... nothing. You just startled me, that's all," I sighed in relief.

"Um, you said come over at eight," she said.

"P. M., Liz. Eight P.M. Why would I ask you to come over at eight A.M.? I work the second shift," I asked in disbelief.

"Hmm, yeah, well I thought that was a little strange," she trailed off.

"Yeah," I spouted.

"Well. What are you up to?"

"Sleeping. I'll see you at eight-fucking-P.M.," I yelled as I walked off.

Townsend

Liz scoffed at me, and I stormed back inside. I think if Anabelle would have awakened, or if Liz would have seen Anabelle, I would have been a goner. I don't want to call that rotten crap a miracle, but, wow. Those two tempers going off at once in that proximity probably would have knocked the earth off its axis and thrown us violently back to the ice-age, where I would have been immediately eaten by a pink dinosaur named Liz. I ended my cheating career that day, and never did it again. I had to pull my shit together. My beating heart may have been spared that day, but not from karma.

My cabby pulled up in front of my apartment, I paid him an enormous tip, hoping to immediately gain better karma. Fifty-plus hours in jail and I had never been so glad to be home. Once inside I hung my hoodie on the coat hook, tossed my keys on the counter and poured some orange juice. The heat was on, so I adjusted the thermostat lower. I rustled my hair and washed my face in the kitchen sink. I fetched my cup of juice and flopped down on the couch.

I was staring into the blank television screen and gulping orange juice when I heard a moan come from the bedroom. Confused, I cautiously approached my bedroom doorway. It was wide open. I peeked around the doorjamb to see Kevin (the Crip thief) and Alec having a threesome with Annabelle, on my own bed. At first, I thought she was being attacked, until she began to laugh. Undetected, I went outside and called another cab.

***

Despite my lawyer's advice, I confided in the person I felt closest to. Matt's mother had put her house up as bond collateral and Matt was now also out on bail. I was getting more and more depressed. I wrecked my first car. The car I fought for hadn't been just a car to me, it made life possible. I was fucked-up depressed. What does the lawyer know? In a time like this I needed friends most. It was not like I had family.

"This is on the house, Brother Miller. Let's just have fun, forget about this life for a while," Matt said as he handed me a pill.

Townsend

We huddled around a space heater in the Bloom family garage that Matt had made in to a make-shift apartment. There, Matt had yet another drug stash and it remained untouched. The guy was like a drug-squirrel. I washed down a pressed Ecstasy pill with a forty-ounce Mickey's. It was only my second time rolling and I thought this was just what I needed. Dr. Bloom advised it. He said I needed to get real and talk it all out with my best friend.

We did. About an hour later we were feeling superb. We chatted about who-knows-what at mile-a-minute. I wanted a family. I wanted to be accepted. I wanted to be liked. I wished my family called to ask how I was. We talked about it all. Matt handed me another free pill, we cheered and washed it down with more Mickey's.

We blabbered for another hour. Another pill.

We were starting to sweat. I noticed Matt's words start to blend together and mumble. Matt was always a great guy to do drugs with. He was on top of things and was a good coach. I wanted to go get more beer, but he turned that idea down and fetched a big jug of water instead. With it we washed another pill down, each.

"Love ya', buddy," I mumbled to Matt.

"Meh, leh, ootoo, mang," Matt mumbled.

I started to freak out. Matt was beyond wide awake but mumbling as if he was heavily sedated.

"Meh?" I asked. I felt my heart jump as I realized I was doing it too.

"Meh…meh…meh…" I mumbled to myself, exaggerating my mouth movements and trying to form words.

"*MEH!*" Matt screamed-mumbled in concern, pointing at my face. Not the best thing to do to someone who is vulnerable and rolling on Ecstasy, to point at them.

"*Meh*, meh?" I mumbled back in high-pitched concern.

We were so messed up that we got in to a rhythm of eating pills. Certain states of inebriation are like insanity, if not a temporary state of exactly that. You look for routine to ground you and feel in control. Part of our routine that night included eating more pills. Matt was dipping into another huge bag of a hundred or so.

Townsend

We were so incredibly lit that we got to the point that we could no longer form words. We were so righteously fucked up we didn't even *realize it*. Matt jabbered on and on until I finally realized we were saying, well, nothing. They call this state "The Mumbles". Although well on my way, my tolerance to substances was still low, all things considered. I hadn't had years to build up a resistance to toxic sludge. Matt jutted a finger at my face, wiped the corner of my mouth, and showed me a bit of my own blood. I buried a finger between my teeth and cheek and pulled it out covered in thick red blood.

"MEH!" Matt panicked.

I ate five triple-stacked pills within the course of a few hours and chewed almost all the way through my own face. I fell to the floor in shock. That was the last thing I remember for a while. Matt went to prison. I went to rehab.

***

WORLDLY

I spent a LONG time recovering. I was lucky to be alive. The physical recovery was brutal. The emotional recovery was worse. For years I could hardly remember what street I lived on. The depression that kind of experience leaves you with is hard to shake. Like so many people in desperate situations, I prayed to God for help. Above all I prayed for faith. I needed the smallest yet unmistakable sign that my prayers were being heard but got nothing more than a dial tone. I was not going to be given an epiphany or miracle, all my lessons were going to be earned the hard way. The damage to my memory and the ability to think clearly were lessons I would carry with me for the better part of ten years.

Really, what happened was a blessing... the pain of my past was duller. My memories just felt as if they were stories told to me, bearing no real emotional attachment. A lot of memories I am left with are just that, stories told to me about what I did. I was lucky my job sent me to a nice rehab facility, but I really wasted it. Even then I was not quite at rock bottom. I was probably the only one in there for Ecstasy. At the time I felt like 'addiction' was a synonym to the word 'fun'. I didn't get much out of rehab but soggy hamburgers and some new connections. I was unreachable through the doctrine of a twelve-step program centered on spirituality. I felt there was

Townsend

no way some generic organization of steps using a higher power as motivation was going to help me. My power came from within and my motivation was learned by practical experience, but I had not collected it all yet.

I did exactly what you should *not* do in that situation: I made friends in rehab. At night we climbed through our windows, snuck out and went out on the town drinking. Most every person in there had something as, or more terrible, happen to them in the past. Those stories are what I was most interested in while in rehab. Human experience is where I collect my data on life, but as humans we kind of tend to dwell on our injustices. It rips us apart. We replay it, over and over. We take a wound and tear it apart by our own hand. My dad was a dick. It broke my heart, but I made it a compound fracture. That story is far from rare. Lemmings off a cliff into a sea of treatment, booze and antidepressants. Cogs in a wheel.

***

Before long I was back home, living with Gianna in Levittown. She took me in once again when I lost my apartment after the mess with Annabelle and my overdose. It was down to just me and Alec now. Matt was upstate in prison. We went to visit him once, but it was all the way up around Binghampton. The one time we tried to visit him was a disaster. Alec had bought a piece of crap 1970's Cadillac he thought was "big pimpin", and the thing caught on fire just forty-five minutes down the road. That was actually my fault; I had changed the oil for the road trip and left a rag on the engine block. It burned to the ground on the side of the Belt Parkway and we had to call my ex-girlfriend, Annabelle, to pick us up. That was a very awkward ride home, considering the last time I'd seen Annabelle she was having sex with Alec.

Our drug use had made a natural progression from uppers to downers and our thing had become pain killers and Xanax. Pain killers… the name just appealed to me, or maybe it was just the notion. We did everything we could do to get ahold of fifteen-milligram Roxies, the addiction came on quick and as strong as a hurricane and did as much damage. I had damaged my vertebra in the accident and was easily able to talk an old doctor in to a new prescription. Alec and I would blow through them in about a week (and then we were hunting for more, at fifteen dollars a pop). Literally blow through them… our thing was to grind up Roxies and Xanax together and snort

Townsend

the mixture. Soon after we found that adding Soma muscle relaxers to the mix made us feel even more incredible.

If you have been hiding under a rock for a number of years, then let me warn you about pain killers. Yes, they made us feel wonderful for three to four hours if we ate them. We felt *really* good for an hour or two if we snorted them. Think of it as a glass full of water. The water represents the amount of happy-go-lucky you have available for your brain to squirt out. Everyone is different, but your brain normally drips it out, drop by drop. Taking pain killers like Vicodin tips the glass to a thin steady pour. Roxies, Oxycontin and heroine pretty much dump the glass over. You feel great for a while, but you quickly need another pill to keep it going. After a while the glass is empty. Your body will fill the glass back up, but in its own time and it can't do it if the glass is already tipped over. We were constantly chasing pills just to feel normal. A lot of the time we were chasing a high we hadn't really felt for months; we were just avoiding illness.

My happiness and my normal came in pill form. When I did not have it, I was a mess. I was irritable and violently ill… dope sick. Saying "yes" and trying this drug was so dangerous because it felt good (for a while) … and it was *immensely* addictive. Little did I know that by just trying this drug I would create a ten-year problem for myself, and as of today one in three American adults of all ages can relate. You can thank the great university-educated drug dealers for that one.

After about a year of ingesting pain killers almost every day I had enough of running out and going into withdrawal. I wanted to try different things and get to know what was out there. I wanted to try everything. The idea of doing the same thing every day as one does in addiction goes against that goal and I'd had enough. I turned off my phone and hunkered down. After twenty-four hours I was crawling out of my skin and I kept picking up my phone like a madman, tempted to give in and call Alec. By the third day I was so sick I could not sit still but could not get out of bed either. I was inconsolably depressed. My legs jumped on their own. I was freezing but soaked the sheets with sweat. A week later I found I could walk to the refrigerator and out to the mailbox.

That night Alec picked me up and the first thing we did was grind up three Roxies and half a Xanax bar. Heath Ledger, Philip Seymour Hoffman and L'il Peep, to name a famous few, have died from the nature of this particular mixture. These drugs are sedatives and slow both breathing

Townsend

and heart rate. Drugs like Xanax and Oxycodone should never be mixed, we did not know that until people we knew started to turn up dead. That night we had already lost one friend and the buzz about a dead celebrity or two had been heard, but we had quickly ignored it.

Opioids have a way of making you rationalize just about anything, as long as it includes more opiates. After a while it will replace the importance of meals. I had gone a full week without any pills and managed to talk myself into celebrating the opiate-free success with… opioids. Alec and I sat in the front seat of his new Cadi… it was a 1983.

"You got a little on your nose," I told Alec.

Alec wiped the pale green mixture onto his hand and licked it clean.

"Back to my house?" Alec asked, and I nodded in approval.

"Thanks man, I feel so much better," I told him.

"No worries, brotha'. I got some K back at the house too!" he said cackling.

WORLDLY

"Oh shit!" I exclaimed.

"K", "Special K" or Ketamine is an animal tranquilizer that does wild things to the human body. In big enough doses it will throw you into a "K-Hole" in which you may have an outer-body experience. It comes in a vial and can either be injected or squirted on to a plate and microwaved into a powder and snorted. Our common K experience included a weightless sensation like we were floating through the air. Matt would describe it as landing on a world made of liquid and having Thanksgiving dinner with extra-terrestrials, but I know he was just lying there staring at the ceiling and drooling. If you did not have a big enough dose for a K-Hole you would at least be stuck, paralyzed in place and out of your mind for five to ten minutes. You usually had to inject the Ketamine to experience the trance of a K-Hole and I would only snort it. I did get to that point once, the first time trying it. I sniffed a line of Ketamine and the corner of the room sniffed me up. My soul sat perched in the corner of the room watching myself for fifteen minutes as Matt was passed out next to me with a needle sticking out of his thigh. I sat up in the ceiling giggling for the duration until the reverse gravity gave way and I fell, smacking hard back into my body. Only at that point was I able to check to make sure Matt was still alive, I needed hands.

"Hey, so I broke up with Nicole." Alec told me.

"What?" I asked. "Why?"

"She is crazy, man. She tried to roofie Matt with GHB, but she did it wrong and asked him if he would like to be roofied," he said.

"Yeah… Nicole did that to me too," I carefully told him.

"Did you fuck her?"

"No man! No way! I don't think GHB would even help. Although I do find it kind of funny that you are worried if I fucked your girlfriend, Alec."

"Oh, yeah…" he said, remembering the hypocrisy.

"GHB wouldn't help because I still wouldn't do it," I said, driving in the last nail before leaving the subject alone.

"I'm still really sorry dude. My bad," Alec apologized.

"It's OK, like I said… I am no prize either… not even mad at her. Is what it is."

"Well, I broke up with Carla. She went ape-shit bro'. I mean, she *lost* it. She even threw a toaster at my head," Alec said showing me a kid's Band-Aid on his forehead.

"Jeez man! What if you have a concussion? Have you been sleepy? Hard to think?" I asked him.

He just looked at me and I realized I had asked a stupid question. Alec pulled over on to a random side street and turned off his lights.

"Well, that's why I really wanted to hang out tonight, B. She's been following me around," he said, and I cocked my head, giving him a shocked look. "Yea Jason, she fuckin *lost* it. I think she is trying to kill me! You think you can kick it with me until she chills out?"

"Yeah man! Of course, we're brothers. I got you," I told him.

"I appreciate you, dawg, seriously."

Townsend

"Plus, I want to see you get your ass kicked by Carla," I said. "I'm ready to take a picture of that shit."

Alec scoffed and socked me in the shoulder. He turned on a map light, so we could see in the dark car. Alec pulled out a little plastic box with a cut-off from a straw. He opened it up and cut out another two pale green lines. These were fat this time. I horked my line and within five minutes was feeling very strange. I was getting woozy. My tolerance had dropped considerably in just a week. Alec finished his line and thumbed his nose.

"Damn dude, I think I put too much Xanax," he said. "I'm fucked up."

"Yea, me too, but I'm not looking to go back to jail tonight. We gotta' be safe, B," I told him.

My head was spinning and fuzzy. I felt tired as hell but on top of the world. I felt like my whole body was wrapped in a warm fuzzy blanket. Alec put on 50 Cent's new album *Get Rich or Die Tryin'* and we sat there listening to it and rapping along for a good thirty minutes. We just sat there in the car by the side of a residential street and hung out... it was fun.

Headlights appeared in front of us as a car turned into the street. Alec perked up and watched the car pass, I was getting increasingly woozier. Alec watched the car pass by, started the Cadi, turned around, and began to carefully follow the car. The car pulled in to a driveway and Alec pulled over, but on the left side of the street as there was no parking on the right. I kept nodding off and catching myself. The car Alec was following turned out to be just turning around in the driveway. When it got closer I recognized it to be Carla's blue Ford Probe.

"Hey! That's Carla!" I slurred and scratched my nose.

I opened my car door as her car flew up on us. Her car smashed into Alec's open passenger door.

"What are you doing?" Alec screamed at me.

The dopey smile faded from my face as I looked at Carla who was screaming at us from a rolled-down window. I realized what I had just done.

"Oh shit," I groaned.

Townsend

Alec floored the accelerator and took off down the street. I heard screeching tires behind us as Carla made a U-turn and sped after us. I suddenly felt like puking. Carla's car was much more maneuverable than Alec's, before long she was right on our tail and furious. She was honking the horn and even rode up on our bumper for a moment. I picked that moment to vomit. I leaned out the moving car window and vomited into the open air. Alec kept the accelerator floored. The wind caught my vomit and it sailed behind us onto Carla's windshield. I saw Carla's eyes widen in disgust.

"Sorry! Sorry..." I yelled back to her while wiping my chin.

We gained some distance from her as she slowed down and put on her windshield wipers. That smeared the bile across her windshield and disabled her vision. In deeply irritated disbelief she smashed the brake pedal and pulled to the side of the road, knocking over a trash can.

"Good job buddy!" Alec cheered as he patted me on the back, which made me dry heave, so he quickly stopped.

WORLDLY

The Cadi pulled back on to Hempstead Turnpike and before long we lost Carla. Later we pulled up to Alec's Levittown apartment. In Levittown there are not many apartment buildings. Levittown was the first suburb in America built for the veterans returning from World War II. There were three styles of homes to choose from and all had postage- stamp lawns. A Levitt-house was said to be built production-line style in a single day and William Levitt built roughly 1,400 in Levittown, New York. Therefore, the apartments for rent there are in family homes. Most homeowners have remodeled to include a small apartment or granny flat to sublet and help cover the nearly six thousand dollars a year in property taxes. Alec's apartment was the whole upstairs level of the house, which had been remodeled as a separate residence.

Alec and I stomped up the deck stairs to his apartment. We hurried inside to find his stash of Ketamine.

"Bust that shit out man! Let's go!" I encouraged Alec.

Alec ran into his bedroom and threw a bunch of stuff around until he emerged with a small glass vial. He came back holding the vial and a syringe and handed it to me. I took the

Townsend

glass plate out of his microwave and set it on the countertop. I poked the syringe into the vial and pulled a full draw of Ketamine. I squirted it onto the glass plate and popped it in the microwave. I cooked it for a minute, pulled the plate back out and handed it to my friend. Alec placed it on top of a burner on the stove and used a flat razor blade from a box knife to scrape up the dried K into lines. He rifled through his cabinets until he found a box of straws. He pulled out two, but they were the kind that bend at the neck. He used scissors to cut the bend off, leaving about four inches of straw. I looked into the box and found a McDonalds straw.

"Oh man, I want this one!" I said.

"Well shit, yeah, me too. I didn't see that one," he responded, and let the bendy straws drop to the ground. His house was a wreck; he just threw most trash right on the floor.

McDonalds straws are the best for snorting drugs. They are wider than most other straws. It's like snorting with a PVC pipe. I cut the McDonalds straw in half and handed him one. We pulled the protective paper off and stood staring at each other, slightly nervous.

"See ya' on the other side, B," Alec told me.

"Yeah buddy," I replied.

I horked a fat line of K and stood there holding my nose for about fifteen seconds until I disappeared holding onto the edge of the stove. Alec pulled the plate to himself and did his line. We both stood there, frozen in place. I clenched onto the stove as the helium started to lift my body from the ground. The K took over my head and I drifted into a trance. Alec stood with his hands raised almost in boxing form, his fists clenched so tight he crushed the straw.

We stood there, not in control of our own frozen bodies. Through clenched teeth I grinned at Alec who was groaning from his high. Ten feet away the kitchen door swung open and there stood Carla, ready to scream at Alec. She was pissed.

"You left your…" Carla started to yell until she laid eyes on us.

She saw immediately that we were standing frozen in place and knew exactly what was happening. She was well aware of Ketamine and knew what state we were in. She smirked and retained an evil grin as she marched towards us.

Townsend

Both of our eyes were as wide as dinner plates as she approached us; we started to panic but could not run. We had no control of our bodies. We felt as if we weighed a thousand pounds. Carla, just to fuck with us (and because she was nuts) got down on her knees in front of Alec and pulled down his sweat pants. I was standing twelve inches away from Alec and was helpless. We just stared at each other with stupid panicked looks. Carla put his limp penis in her mouth. Alec scraped up the ability to flop a hand onto my arm and clenched my hoodie.

"H-hhhhhelp-p… m-mmmmmmeeeee!" he groaned through his teeth like the living dead.

I did not know what to do, at that moment we were prisoners in our own bodies. I groaned in anger, desperately fighting to get control of my body.

"Nnnnuuuuhhhhhh!" I groaned through gritted teeth and threw my weight into Alec.

We both stumbled, and I stepped on Carla as our weight turned into momentum. We stumbled further a few feet and slammed into a wall.

"You fucking *pricks*!" Carla yelled, slightly angry that she had just been trampled over.

I now threw my weight to the right, dragging Alec by the shoulders towards the first opening, the bedroom. He tripped on his sweatpants that were around his ankles and we both fell into the bedroom. I heard Carla running toward the bedroom and I kicked the door closed just as she tried to enter. The door bounced off her face and the adrenaline rush gave me enough dexterity to reach up and lock the handle. Carla began to pound on the door. The Ketamine was starting to wear off, it only lasted ten minutes or so and after that I was able to get back on my feet and look out of Alec's bedroom window. I saw that the awning for the first-floor front door was below us. I pushed the screen out and reached over to grab Alec. He was also coming out of his high and was pulling up his pants. We both sat on the edge of the window sill, jumped onto the awning and then to the front yard.

"Please tell me you have your keys." I asked Alec.

"Shit! Shit, I think I left them in the door!" he screamed at me.

Townsend

Without hesitating, I sprinted around the back of the house and up the stairs to his front door, slowing at the top three steps. Carla had closed the door behind her and I saw Alec's keys hanging from the deadbolt. I approached slowly, standing on my tip toes to see through the front door window. I saw Carla still attempting to break down Alec's bedroom door. She was now throwing her body weight into the hollow-core door. This brought me déjà vu. I knew without anyone countering the impact from the other side, she would eventually succeed. At that moment however, she was occupied, so I easily walked up and removed Alec's keys from the deadbolt of the front door. I sprinted away as fast as my legs could carry me. Alec and I jumped in to the Cadi and sped away as Alec received a phone call.

"There's a party in Wantagh," he told me after ending the call.

"Thank God, let's forget about this shit," I responded. "Let's go."

Once in Wantagh we realized the scale of the party we were about to attend by the lack of parking on the street. It was a house I did not know. This gave me the jitters. Since leaving home and entering the real world I was always apprehensive about new people, it is something hard to shake. It goes against my goal of who I want to be, but there is something deeply engrained in my psyche that tells me to be wary. I am introverted trying very hard to be an extrovert. Alec knew this about me and knew that I would have a hard time for about the first hour of the party until I met some people and warmed up. So, he had his prescription ready... more Xanax. Alec presented his box of drugs yet again and we snorted more of the Xanax-heavy mixture of oxycodone. I think that was the line that did me in- or possibly the addition of liquor once we went inside.

I came to on Matt's older brother's couch. I remember stepping out of the haze and at first not recognizing where I was or any of the unfamiliar faces that surrounded me. There was a smaller party in progress when I came to, but it was at a different home. I approached someone sitting nearby and leaned in close to their face, invading his personal space.

"Who-who are you?" I asked groggily.

The person just laughed as if I was joking. It was Carla's brother and he knew me very well, being Alec's best friend and all. Ricardo was a nice guy but an introvert- so he liked me. He wanted to be better friends than I did with him as I really wanted to surround myself with extroverts. I had no need to spend my valuable free time on a couch playing video games. At that moment though, I had no idea who he was.

"Yeah, alright man," he laughed.

I gave him a tragically confused look and his amusement faded when he realized I was in fact not joking.

"It's me… Ricardo, Jason," he responded, this time with concerned seriousness. "Here sit down next to me bro'."

Ricardo pulled me by the elbow, I lost my balance and flopped down on the couch next to him. As I looked around my senses started to flood back to me and I began to recognize the room I was in. It was like blood rushing back into a foot after it had fallen asleep, only it was my brain. I turned to stare at Ricardo; he stared back, giggling uncomfortably.

"R-Ricardo!" I yelled in his face.

"Yeah-yeah bro'! Damn! Geez what a relief… you were *really* fucked up!"

I looked around, frantically scanning for more clues. My face lit up when recognition finally began to come.

"We-we're at David's!" I yelled again in Ricardo's face, having a hard time controlling my volume. "This is David *Bloom's* house!"

"Yeah!" Ricardo cheered and ruffled my hair. "Fuck yeah, it is!"

Now that my consciousness had come back I started to evaluate what led me to this position. I felt as if I was just coming out of a coma, or, gaining back my sanity.

"Fuck. What happened to me?"

"I dunno' man. You have been fucked up for a long time, really fucked up. I dunno' if I have ever seen someone so fucking gone. Everyone here has been keeping an eye on you... in shifts," he answered. "We were hoping we didn't have to take you to the hospital."

"Shifts? How long has it been?"

Townsend

"Uh, I mean I just got here two days ago but from what I've heard- you have been out of it for like three days."

"Wh-where is Alec? I asked looking around.

"He left you," Carla answered as she entered the room.

I felt alarmed to be in Carla's presence. Ricardo and Carla were often mutually exclusive, they did not care for each other very much and I had assumed Carla would not be there since Ricardo was.

"Alec got scared and thought you were going to die or something, so he left you alone at a party in Wantagh and took off," she said.

"How did you…" I began.

"Well, you were trying to fuck my friend Jennifer and you told her about the car chase between me and Alec. She called me to come get you before you got your ass kicked by her boyfriend," she replied, cutting me off.

I buried my face in my hands, beginning to feel really embarrassed.

"I-I'm sorry…" I said as I groaned into my palms.

"It's OK. Ricky and I were really worried about you. We came as soon as we heard," she said.

"It's OK man. We got you," Ricardo said and patted me on the back.

"Alec is a real fuckwit, bro', Carla said. "He doesn't give a shit about you."

"As soon as you became a liability he dumped you like a bad habit," Ricardo told me.

I could not think of any other "bad habits" Alec had yet dumped. I had soon realized that it was four in the morning when I came to. Everyone around me had been up all night and I was just waking up. I spent a couple hours getting my bearings when Ricardo said he had enough of partying and wanted to go home. Carla was drunk but after a few sobriety tests she offered her car if I would drive Ricardo home and come straight back. I welcomed the change of scenery and the car ride.

Townsend

In a strange turn of events, it was I that ended up driving the blue Ford Probe a few days after fleeing from it and opening a Cadillac door into it. It was not as if the car was in perfect condition. Carla never washed it and the clear coat had faded. The front license plate was hanging by a single tired bolt. Still, upon approaching it I quickly saw the evidence of what I had been partially responsible for. The front bumper cover was cracked, and a mirror was knocked off and hanging by a wire harness. It was my job to assess car accidents and upon seeing the damage I recalled exactly how it had happened. I groaned quite loudly when I saw it, it now looked twice as dilapidated.

"Yeah, you had a busy week, huh?" Ricardo asked with a chuckle.

"God damn dude," I replied as I trudged over to the driver's door and got in.

Ricardo lived at home with his parents in Queens. It was a forty-minute drive to get there, mostly highway. We jumped on the Southern State to the Van Wyck ready to haul ass but was quickly disappointed as we realized it was rush hour.

"Hey... Ricardo?" I asked hesitantly. "What day is it?"

"Umm... today is... Tuesday. Wednesday? No... it's Tuesday."

My heart sank again realizing I had missed two days of work. I groaned again, loudly. Ricardo looked over at me feeling weird that I was freaking out.

"Hey man, whatever it is there is nothing you can do about it right now, so don't beat yourself up. Wanna' smoke?" he asked.

You know, I think a lot of people who have made lousy decisions (that I know) really did not know that their choices were so bad when they were making them. I did not have that excuse. Every time I did something stupid I had ignored a little voice inside telling me not to do it.

"Sure, let's smoke."

It had taken me some time to realize and feel what my body was doing again, but it had been some time since I had any opioids. I was starting to feel really bad again and the marijuana would surely help take my mind off it. Ricky pulled

Townsend

out a little ceramic one-hitter that was painted to look like a cigarette. He loaded a pinch of pot into the end of it. We were now in bumper-to-bumper traffic in a sea of cars, so I was glad his piece looked like a cigarette. In those days having marijuana was just about as a bad as having cocaine so it was best to think ahead. Ricardo offered me the pipe.

"Hold on a sec..." I said as I checked the car's one good mirror.

From the lane we were traveling in we had traffic along both sides of us. I decided it best to reduce the risk of being seen by half and get over one lane to the far right. I seized the opportunity to get over when a driver took an extra second to move up, allowing me to dart into the right lane in front of him. Once in the far-right lane, I only had traffic beside me to my left. I accepted the pipe and lit the end, taking a long drag. As I exhaled I blew out of the driver's window where I locked eyes with a uniformed police officer in an unmarked Crown Victoria. His windows were rolled up and could not smell the smoke, so I was confident. I even held the ceramic "cigarette" out of the car window as if I was only smoking a cigarette. The Crown Victoria quickly moved up in traffic and out of sight.

Woop, woop! – The sound of a police car chirped from behind us. I jumped out of my skin.

"Shit, shit shit!" I screamed.

"Calm down man, it's alright. It's Carla's car and you have permission. Everything is going to be fine," Ricky said as he calmly put his ceramic one hitter into a pack of Parliaments.

I pulled over to the shoulder with a Highway Patrol car lit up behind me. I felt my pockets and realized I had no clue where my wallet was. I watched a police officer approach the driver's window through my one good wing mirror. I kept my hands on the steering wheel and a smile on my face. Just then the weed started to kick in and I wished it had not. My hands got pale and clammy and started to shake.

"Hello officer," I greeted the policeman.

"Do you know why I pulled you over?" he said, ignoring the greeting.

Townsend

"No- no I sure don't," I replied with a shaking voice. I wondered if he could smell the marijuana. "I don't think I was speeding."

The officer looked at me as if I had a mental problem, and then and the crawling traffic behind him.

"No, you weren't speeding..." he said very seriously.

I wriggled in my seat, feeling an itch and trying not to move. I thought again of the T-Rex in Jurassic Park- maybe if I stayed absolutely still I would disappear from his sight.

"You are however, driving with a broken rearview mirror, a broken bumper and an improperly secured license plate...driver's license and registration please," he continued very sternly.

Not having my wallet was not the worst of the problem with my driver's license. I did not have a valid license. Part of my deal in my last problem with the law was that I gave up my driving privilege for five years.

"Well... here's the problem," I started.

The officer cocked his head and was now irritated knowing I was about to follow up with something even more irritating.

"I forgot my wallet at home and this is my friend's car."

"This is my sister's car, sir; he is just taking me home. He has permission. He is the designated driver. We can call her," Ricardo said.

"Designated driver? It's morning rush hour... so you don't have any identification?" he asked.

"No sir, I'm sorry," I replied.

"OK, well, look in the glove box and see if the papers are in there," he said, exasperated.

Ricardo and I sprang to life, dug through the glove box and center console looking for the insurance and registration papers. The officer kept his palm on his holstered weapon. We turned up nothing and shrugged to the police officer giving our best sheepish looks.

Townsend

"Alright, well what's your name? I can run your plate for the rest," he said, and I sensed he was really trying to work with us.

"Matt Bloom, sir," I said, and Ricardo looked over at me with a stupid look, luckily the officer did not notice it.

"Birth date?" he asked.

I panicked a second but remembered the huge party we had for him just before he went away. It was a birthday party.

"November tenth," I answered.

"…and the year?" he asked.

He was not leaving anything to chance, geez. Matt was a year older than me.

"1982," I replied.

The officer finished writing on a pad.

"OK. Wait here until I come back. I am going to run all of this; it will probably take a few minutes. Turn off the car," he told us as he walked towards his squad car parked a good fifteen yards behind us.

"Dude! What the fuck? You just gave him the name of someone who is currently in prison!" Ricardo snarled.

"Fuck. I dunno' man! That's the only birthday I could think of! Does Carla have fuckin' insurance?" I snarled back.

"No! She doesn't, or her car would be in the fuckin' shop right now because you smashed it!"

"Fuck!" I yelled in a frustrated whisper.

Instead of turning off the ignition I slammed the car into drive and punched the accelerator. The shoulder ended a few yards ahead of me. Our sudden movement scared one of the slow drivers and he braked, allowing us to jump in front of him.

"DUDE! What the fuck are you doing?" Ricardo screamed at the top of his lungs.

"Shit, shit, *shit*!" I answered.

Townsend

I drove the Ford Probe up close to the bumper of the car in front of me and frantically looked for quicker ways forward. We advanced a quarter of mile down the road. I checked the mirrors for the police car and saw nothing. I was long past where the shoulder had ended and the only way the car could pursue me was through heavy rush-hour traffic. I heard a siren come on from a few cars behind us but still could not see it. Ricardo turned around looking out of the back window and also could not spot the police car in the traffic. A sign for the Valley Stream exit came up just as the shoulder returned. I knew if I did not take it the police car would soon catch up. I got onto the shoulder and sped towards the exit at about forty-miles-per-hour while the traffic to the left crawled along.

Before long I was exited off into the Valley Stream neighborhood and took a bunch of turns down winding streets until I was lost, hoping I had shaken the police car. I parked under a thick maple tree and stopped, putting the car in park. I finally peeled my foot off the car's pedals and it jumped like a fish being pulled out of a stream. My heart pumped like an oil well. Ricky was frantically looking all around the car.

"Holy shit! I think you did it!" he screamed and laughed hysterically.

I exhaled deeply and allowed myself a small chuckle in sweet relief.

"Oh, fuck man. If we got caught, we were going away." I told him. "We are going to have to take back roads the rest of the way to Forest Hills. Do you know how to get there?"

"Oh, fuck no… I'm taking the bus the rest of the way," he stated firmly.

"I'm sorry," I said.

"No man, you got us out of it, it's cool! I can't believe we got away but I'm not pressing my luck any further. I'm taking the bus," he said as he got ready to get out of the car.

"Well that's a smart move," I replied.

"No worries man, you just get back safe, and get out of this car. Maybe you should just ditch it and take the bus too."

"Ah shit man, I have to get Carla her car back."

Townsend

"So, what? She can get a ride and come pick it up later if the cops don't, bro'. You've been through enough, don't push it any further. This car is a worthless piece of shit anyway."

"Still worth more than I am. I smash up her car, you guys still rescue me and then I turn around and lose her car?" I said. "She will fucking kill me if I don't bring it back. Queens Boulevard turns into Hempstead Turnpike, right?"

"You're crazy man...I would not take it...it will be littered with cops. But yeah, Queens Boulevard turns into Hempstead Turnpike."

I don't know why I didn't just take the bus back to Levittown. If I am really honest- I think I just was not ready for the thrill to end. I wanted more and had not yet exhausted my supply of stupid. I avoided the Southern State Parkway but still chose to take a major roadway back to Levittown... because it was quicker. I do not know how, but I made it back to David Bloom's without even *seeing* a single cop. Maybe the police officer never called it in, maybe he didn't want to deal with it.

WORLDLY

When I got back to David's everyone was half awake, tuckered out from a full night of partying. They were too tired to hear the story of what happened. No one really believed me until a few days later when Ricardo reiterated the story. He thought I was Al Capone. Carla sold the Ford Probe the next day for five-hundred dollars, just to get rid of it. Once back at David's house I took a yellow-cab back to the serenity of Gianna's apartment. She was gone to work, and I flopped down on the couch and slept like a baby for four hours.

When I woke up I showered and decided I would show up for work. I was yet again happy that I worked the second shift. As I drove Gianna's spare car to work I worried what I would tell my supervisor, to my knowledge I had not called in sick, but then again, I could not remember if I had. I thought if I walked in and everyone asked if I was doing better than I must have called in sick. If I walked in and got a bunch of dirty looks from people who had to pick up my slack- then I was a no call/no show for two whole scheduled days of work and would consequently shit my pants like a rhinoceros.

The latter became quickly evident. I walked to my desk testing the regular acquaintances with a smile and universally getting nothing but confusion or frustrated looks in return.

Townsend

That night I picked a cubicle more towards the nucleus of the call-center, hoping to make my presence known as part of the team. I set my backpack down and sat in the desk chair. I had a few minutes until sign-in, you had to sign in exactly on the hour, not a minute off. I signed into my computer and it loaded my personal desktop design. No matter what desk you sat at the computer would always pull up your personal Windows desktop upon sign in. My desktop picture was of a large commercial building on the top of a large hill surrounded by palm trees. It was the company's San Diego office. I sat in silence and stared longingly at the picture on my computer screen. I sighed and was thinking about how much trouble I was in when I felt a hand on my shoulder.

"Jason!" a stern male voice greeted.

I jumped and turned around, it was my boss, Mr. Schweitzer.

"H-hello sir! How are you?" I asked nervously.

"Let's have a chat before you sign into that phone, shall we?" he answered.

I was confused. His tone sounded cheerful, but his words were stern. I got up and followed him to his cubicle. He moved fast and was sitting by the time I reached his desk.

"Have a seat there, Mr. Miller," he instructed.

"Sure!" I said, sounding like a nervous brown-nose.

Mr. Schweitzer leaned back in his office chair and fiddled with a fancy pen in his hand while staring me down. I shifted in my seat.

"I'm not going to lie; I am pretty damn surprised to see *you* back here," he said with an undertone of exasperation that both shocked and frightened me.

"Umm…" I started trying to find an explanation, but I really did not remember what happened in the past few days so little explanation could be given.

"I have several employees that say you came in for your shift drunk two nights ago."

Townsend

I looked at him in complete shock, unable to respond. My throat made a little squeaking sound as I started to respond without first having a word ready to form.

"It took three of them to get you to leave. You were…" he paused as he looked at a few pages stapled together on a clipboard. That was when I realized I had been written up and there was a permanent record of this.

"… inebriated and belligerent."

Apparently even in my "inebriated and belligerent" three-day trance I still had remembered to show up for work. My survival instincts had transcended intoxicated stupor. Unfortunately, I was not exactly low-key and was pretty much immediately removed from the building. My heart sank- that job was the only bit of stability I had in my life. I wondered what I would do if I lost my job.

"What's going on with you, Jason? Are you in trouble?" Mr. Schweitzer asked.

I sat and thought hard about that question. I thought about how my definition of trouble had changed. I felt I was in trouble when I lived at home and was constantly forced into religious slavery. That was no longer the case, I was New York free, but in a new kind of trouble. I had no one to lift me up when I started to drown, and I was swallowing water. I had experienced too much too fast. I had only graduated high school four years ago. That was the case with all my ex-Jehovah's Witness friends. We tried too hard to be part of the world that we were no longer treading water. Hubert was dead, Matt was in prison upstate, Alec was not exactly doing well, and these were my friends. I had realized you are what you eat, and I fled to New York just to eat out of the same soup bowl. I was not surrounded by people who were stronger than me. I was surrounded by people who were in the same boat as I was, and we were all going down with the ship. I saw the rest of my life going that way. I developed a fully-formed phobia, right there in my chair, of ending up forever a failure.

"Yes. I am," I responded to Mr. Schweitzer.

I cleared my throat and squirmed some more. My eyes welled up as I had just bared a deeply honest truth that I had not before allowed myself to realize. I spent all my effort to avoid thinking about that outcome, ending up nothing- just as my parents hoped I would, proving their predictions correct

Townsend

about me. Mr. Schweitzer looked at me as he would a son. He squirmed in his seat and leaned in with concern.

"You can talk to me, Jason. What is it?"

"I need to leave New York."

Mr. Schweitzer's body language shifted from concern to defense. Without him even saying a word I knew this was not something he would support. He leaned back in his chair and folded his arms.

"What do you mean leave New York? What kind of timeframe are we talking? You are a part of a team here Jason and our call percentages are suffering lately. We can't afford to lose anyone. This company has great resources, maybe there is something we can help with."

"What I need is to start over, Mr. Schweitzer. I messed New York up."

"What do you mean you messed New York up? Look son, I have lived in this town my entire life. If you think my whole life has been easy, psh, forgetaboutit. Now look at me, I've got three kids, a wife and this job. It doesn't pay too bad, bro'. I can at least afford a mortgage and these insane property taxes. You have to stay put and build resources. A man doesn't run from his problems. He stays put and digs his heels in. Grab the bull by the fuckin' horns kid."

All I could think about was a clean slate. He could see in my face that I had received little comfort from his advice. You have to be very stubborn to end up in my various precarious positions.

"Well, where do you want to go, Jason?" Mr. Schweitzer asked.

"San Diego... I'd like to transfer to the office there." I said. Saying it out loud solidified the idea. That's how I was and still am. That's how I finished this book. If I get something in my head, I cannot rest until it is done. It all starts by saying it out loud to someone and then I don't shut up about it until it is done. The San Diego idea kind of matured right there in that moment, and it was there to stay.

Mr. Schweitzer opened his desk drawer and pulled out a form from a hanging folder.

Townsend

"Well, we can get the ball rolling on that, sure. It's not going to happen overnight, Jason. I will fill out this recommendation if you start turning your numbers around. This is probably at least a three-month process. You gotta' go online onto the job board and see if there's any positions available, apply, and they will vet you and contact me if they are interested," he started.

My heart sank further. I was thinking more like the end of the week, as if my company had a fucking witness protection program or something.

"In the meantime, we are going to make a performance improvement plan for you, bud. You want that transfer recommendation then you're gonna' do *better* than the minimum stats. So, we're going to do a review right now," Schweitzer rolled on, instantly clinching his leverage. From a company standpoint, he was a damn good manager.

He put his pen down on the clipboard and found his place in what looked like a long line of questioning.

"Any time there is an incident report we have to do a drug test, so I'll give you one more day before I file this to let the alcohol out of your system. Then they are going to want a hair sample down in medical," he said, seemingly confident I would pass.

I turned white and quietly panicked which was preceded by a small fart as I lost all hope. It was like every hope I had of keeping my job just puffed away into thin air leaving nothing but a foul odor- which would also quickly disappear, forgotten.

"OK, Jason… this is just a side note here but one of the other claims examiners said that you asked if you could "clock in before you leave" … why would you ask to do that? This isn't something you have done before is it?" he asked driving me in to full, uncontrollable panic.

I was now worried that they would check the security cameras and see me leaving several shifts to go party and coming back to clock out. That was the absolute last straw, the proverbial nail in the coffin. So, I did what anyone would do. I jumped on top of the empty desktop in the cubicle in front of Mr. Schweitzer's and leaned down to him from up high. Just then one of my favorite movie scenes from college popped in to my head and I seized the opportunity.

Townsend

"Fuck you…" I told him as I jutted a finger in his direction. He sat speechless and staring back at me as if I had just shot him in the chest. Then I turned to scan the other cubicles in which most of the employees were now telling their customers to 'hold on' and staring at me.

"… fuck you, fuck you, fuck you…" I said pointing to the employees I thought had ratted on me. I then came to a little old lady that had been very nice to me and who currently looked terrified. "…You're cool… I'm out!" I shouted as I finished a line from *Half Baked*.

I jumped down from the desk, grabbed my backpack and left the building with a stupid smile and the same sense of adventure I'd felt when fleeing Pennsylvania. It too was getting addictive.

WORLDLY

CHAPTER EIGHT

Flee Until You Reach the Sea

I did it, without even thinking about it. Sometimes that's the easiest way to do it. If you think about it too much you get emotional and it only makes things more difficult, and it does not serve your end-game. I left pretty much everything I had and took off across the country. I ran as far away from New York as I could until I hit the ocean in San Diego. Some friends who had successfully transferred from New York to California already had heard about the spectacle I had made and found it funny enough to be curious and invite me to stay with them for a while. When I got to California I started doing what I enjoyed again- building... and drinking.

I spent years drinking my life away with friends I made in California. Again, I worked to fuel my social life and I drank to make my social life feel fluid. I kept searching. I

Townsend

hoped every night I went out that I would be drunk enough to have the balls to impress the perfect girl. I drove on my suspended license and got pulled over several times, let go every time due to a glitch in inter-state computing.

San Diego is home to several major universities and therefore is quite the party town. I was not in college, but I attended all the parties. People liked hearing my stories as once again I tried to wash them away in a sea of alcohol. Now everyone wanted me to say the word "chawclat" as I now had a New York accent to get rid of. Some people keep their regional accents for life, but not me. I have always tried so hard to fit in that my accent will genuinely shift after a few years in that region. I did not want to be different, you could say it was counted among my phobias. I made a whole new group of friends, this time no ex-Jehovah's Witnesses.

At twenty-six years old I met my wife. We met on a dating website and I was initially resistant to meeting her as it said she was based in New York, I had left New York and had not planned on returning. She was persistent we meet as she was coming to San Diego on business. When I met her, I learned that she was a truly beautiful person who resembled Michelle Rodriguez, and was a flight attendant originally from Puerto Rico. She spoke six languages and mostly worked international flights. She deeply satisfied my curiosity for learning new things and I fell madly in love with her. While we were dating I found out she cheated on me with some guy in New York and I broke up with her. That lasted about a month and when I saw her again I asked her to marry me.

Maria and I got married in a gaudily famous chapel in Las Vegas. We picked Wedding Package No. 2 with seating for thirty in the smaller chapel (we had three guests), twenty-five pictures and a bouquet of six roses. Twelve was not available without an upgrade. We also opted out of having the late Elvis Presley perform the ceremony. We had known each other for eight months.

My overall drug use had faded by moving (except the ones that came with a prescription), but my drinking persisted and was a concern for Maria. I tried to keep it fairly under control when she was home. She was only home half the time. She would book all of her trips in a row, so she would only have to commute to and from JFK once a month from San Diego. That meant I retained half of my bachelor life (without the women). For two weeks out of the month I was ass-up in vat of booze and doing whatever I wanted with friends. For

Townsend

the other two weeks I would disappear and be a married man, doing married things… like making use of a season pass to the San Diego Zoo. My friends knew if I didn't pick up the phone, Maria was back in town.

Being married to a flight attendant can be lonely at times but it also has a way of keeping the relationship fresh. As soon as we missed each other unbearably she would be home. As soon as we got on each other's nerves she was off to work. This made things harder though if she left during a fight, with two weeks left to reconcile in person. She was a very sexual person and two weeks without was hard to do. I did not feel the absence as much because I was usually sedated and on pain killers when she was gone, but it took its toll and we tried using pornography and video-chat-sex to compensate.

It is hard being a partner to someone who has no family. As their partner you become their whole family. I had my bad days when no amount of alcohol could quell the sorrow of missing my mother. Sometimes panic attacks would hit me so hard I could not speak or move for over an hour. I would ask Maria just to scratch my back, but she never really understood how this would help. Maria was my family, but she was also often gone. Luckily, I had adopted family all over the country.

WORLDLY

There were the obvious benefits of being married to an airline employee. I was able to fly back to New York whenever I wanted. As an airline spouse you fly non-rev (non-revenue) or free if there is an unsold seat available. An airline employee gets a set amount of buddy passes, usually six, also good to hand out to friends and family for a free flight but it is lowest priority seating. As a non-rev spouse, I flew at the same priority as the actual airline employee and got the best seat available, often first class. I went back to New York almost every weekend for a while to see Gianna and other friends.

Travel is a hands-on education; hence the reason school field trips exist. I was always interested in seeing how other people live and interpret life but was previously too poor to do so. I have found most racist people I am familiar with are not well-traveled, live in the town they grew up in, and somehow believe they got lucky enough to be born into the most superior town in the world. In the words of Mark Twain: "Travel is fatal to prejudice, bigotry and narrowmindedness, and many of our people need it sorely on these accounts".

I loved the opportunity to travel and stir up the stagnant pool of everyday monotony. Maria and I went to Dublin,

Townsend

Ireland, together- for free. We spent our honeymoon in the Temple Bar district that puts San Diego's drinking problem to shame. We had a private room in a hostel and I spent very little time in it. I was in heaven in Dublin. I stumbled from pub-to-pub with my wife as I collected strange looks. I was dressed like Bam Margera and may as well have been wearing the American flag as a robe. My wife really baffled everyone as I do not think too many Puerto Ricans have made it to Ireland. Everywhere I went someone wanted to buy us a drink and talk about Obama. I was addicted to the friendly and talkative Irish and wanted to have a beer with everyone I saw. My wife did not have the drinking stamina I had, so I would take her back to the hostel and lie with her until she fell asleep. Then I would continue on pub-crawl alone. Our honeymoon may have been her first clue she had made a mistake, she was a smart person, and it did not take long.

We also went to Tokyo, Japan for free. The flight to Japan was fourteen hours long. It was so long that I got drunk *twice* on the way there. We traveled there in the Airbus- a double-decker aircraft with the entire top floor being first class. Maria had to work the flight down in economy while I drank for free and slept in my leather lay-flat seat.

WORLDLY

When the other flight attendants know a spouse is on board they just keep bringing you free things all flight long. This was something I tried to take gracefully but was silently in shock, having never been first class in anything. Nearing the country, I looked at my personal TV screen and learned that most of the Japanese brand names I knew were cities there. When landing at Narita airport I experienced what most aptly feels like landing on an alien planet. Everything was different. The respect people treated you with was alien to the U.S. Even the police officer who kindly approached "randomly" and asked me to write down where I would be staying and for how long in broken English was overly nice about it. Some things about Japan were just inexplicably different- like vending machines that featured life-sized images of Tommy Lee Jones trying to sell you fruit drinks. It was there I got a sense of how different cultures can evolve, but yet be somehow the same. The things you notice right away are surface differences, at the core Japan is no different than the U.S. or Ireland- it is just full of people living, eating, working and trying to explain why we are here. My wife and I visited a temple and I saw things older than I had ever seen which put perspective on my place in time. We peeked in on some monks praying inside a temple which was quite a sight

Townsend

to see up close. I thought of how modern my family's religion seemed in that moment (not a good thing)...but also how superficial it was. Just by poking my head in the door I felt as if I was poking my head through a wormhole very far back in time. I think Maria enjoyed that trip a bit more than others as there were fewer opportunities for me to drink and waste my experience.

CHAPTER NINE

The Reunion

Maria came from a Catholic Puerto Rican family. Family is very important in her culture and she had a hard time understanding the situation with my family. I noticed her start to get cold feet the moment we began talking about having children. Our family structure would be extremely weak, and we would basically be raising children alone with no family members to help. Her family was back in Guaynabo, Puerto Rico, and even if we moved back to Pennsylvania my family was... well, my family. Maria had been daydreaming online over pictures of Lancaster County, Pennsylvania, and was becoming convinced that we would love it there, and that my family would come around. I did not share her optimism, but I entertained it.

Townsend

Around this time an invitation showed up in my email for my ten-year high school reunion. Naturally I was very curious as to what Lancaster had become in my ten-year absence. I tried my best to forget about it for a very long time. Even though I now considered myself a citizen of the world, it was once my home and a part of me (a part I had tried to kill) and I still missed the place. If Maria really wanted to move there and it seemed viable, we would consider it. I responded that I would go to the reunion. To my surprise, my parents welcomed the idea of my new wife and I coming for a visit. It is sinful for a Jehovah's Witness to consider marrying outside of the religion, but once it is done, there is no going back. Divorce is one of the worst things imaginable to a JW, that and homosexuality. So, my parents agreed to let me come home, after twelve years, for a visit. In that time, I had not seen them once. As the day approached Maria became more excited, and I became more frightened.

I had to travel to Pennsylvania first as Maria was working a flight coming back from Spain. My palms sweated the whole flight to Harrisburg Airport as I redundantly ran the situation over and over in my head like a schizophrenic mathematician. I remember walking through the airport and looking for my father. When I first saw him, we did not recognize each other, we had to call on the phone to find each other's location, but we were both right there. I did my best not to cry when I saw him. When I left him, he was intimidating and stocky with dark hair. The man I saw standing in the airport was not the man I remembered. The man in the airport was a frail, shaking old man with gray hair and a limp. It was one of the most scarring experiences of my life, only that one realization... that the old man in front of me really *was* my father. The penalty we paid was evident by the age our bodies wore. Everyone wishes at some point in their life that they had a time machine, I prayed for one but received the opposite.

Seeing my mother again brought tears, lots of them. The only way I had survived until then was by pretending this was not real, that she did not exist. But now, there she was, right in front of me. I hugged her and cried until she pretended it was all OK and took me to the living room. She still remembered what would make me feel better, she scratched my back and I suddenly came back to earth.

For as many days as I was there, in the home I grew up in, that was time spent in the most vulnerable and hidden recesses of my being. As cliché as it is to say: it was pouring

Townsend

salt into an open wound. Besides our introduction however, I would keep these feelings also hidden, for some hope of normalcy during this multifaceted reunion. I went to a meeting with them and fixed some things around the house, but my smoking (even though I hid outside to do it) and worldly ideas did not go over well with them. My parents were also not keen on the idea of me attending the reunion, although by now they knew I was as worldly as anyone who would be there. For them they were fielding a danger to themselves, and did their best to stay at arm's length, even under the same roof. My sister came to visit also, and I overheard my dad advising her not to go out with us, that I was a danger to her.

The reunion itself was dull to most who attended because they saw each other often. To me it was a trip. I had forgotten most of the people there, but it was worth going for the few that I did see. I of course got to play the part of the guy who had gotten out. Kids who had once mocked me for being a weird, sheltered religious kid were now jealous of my life. Most of them married young and had large litters of children. I was married to a beautiful flight attendant that they probably all wished they had. No one there could believe that I had traveled 3,000 miles for that night (and for free), so I had to reiterate my story over and over. No one there could believe how my family relationship, that lady who would come speak to the class, turned out to be. It was a good night, I promised to keep in touch with some people, some said they would love to visit but had no idea when they could afford to do so. By now all of them have fallen back to the same status as before, forgotten.

The next morning Maria and I woke up to my mother standing over us yelling. We had taken the fold-out couch in the family room. She was screaming and crying.

"You are going to *die*, Jason! Don't you *care*?" she screamed.

Maria rolled over to me with a panicked and confused look on her face. It was the kind of look I assume someone who witnessed the impact of United Airlines Flight 175 would have. It is no way to be awakened.

"You have to make things right with Jehovah!" she cried and ran away.

I later found out that a brother in my parent's congregation, Greg Long's father, had passed away that

Townsend

morning. I think that was the moment my wife finally realized what I had been telling her about my family all along, and that there would be no "normal family" involving them.

CHAPTER TEN

Divorce

I have to give Maria credit, she hung in there and collected red flags for a while before she met someone else. A few months later in California I expected her home from her trips but had not received a call from her. A whole week went by and she still was not home, I could not get anyone to find her and she would not call. After a week went by she called me and explained that she was moving back to New York and wanted a divorce. Also, that week my car decided to explode. This caused me to collapse into a black hole. I was already enough of a wreck to push away my wife, now I had that reality to digest. This was most likely the first time I seriously considered suicide. Luckily my buddy Joey hooked me up with his 1991 Ford Bronco so that I was still mobile (I attempted to make him payments). Even having the transportation fixed, it is insanely frustrating having your wife

Townsend

leave you and having no idea where she currently is in the world (or more specifically who she is with).

I soon got a call from another friend I had made in San Diego. Timothy and I had known each other since the day I arrived in San Diego, I met him and his roommate at a bar. We were drinking buddies while he finished his political-science degree at The University of San Diego and I joined him at parties. We had our own summer of '69, in 2006. I had moved on to Tim's couch and we spent each and every summer day waking up around noon, hitting Burger King and the liquor store, and making our way down to Pacific Beach to drink on the sand. We made the most of that summer and it was a good thing, the next summer would be the last summer you could consume alcohol on the beaches of San Diego. Tim and I were there that following summer when a riot broke out on the beach subsequently causing alcohol to be banned.

On Labor Day of 2007 there were masses of people with kegs of beer and everyone was drinking and partying on Pacific Beach. A couple of girls walked by and decided to stop to do lines of coke off my thigh. Tim and I were walking back from the bathroom to our spot in a sea of people on the beach. We squinted trying to find a familiar landmark as a bearing when we noticed objects flying from the beach towards the boardwalk. Thirty seconds later police sirens rang and police officers on ATV's flew towards the crowds. The few objects then looked like the scene opening the movie Gladiator- when so many arrows were shot into the air that they blocked out the sun. Tim and I decided it best to make a sharp left and head to the car instead. Apparently, some drunk college kids got mad at a police officer and threw a bottle. Then everyone started to do it. Now you can no longer drink on the beach in San Diego.

Several years later Tim got serious with a girl he met at a party in San Diego and he moved with her to Dallas, Texas, to take a job as a grocery store manager. When Maria left me, (or rather decided not to come home) Tim invited me to come to Dallas and get my mind out of the turmoil it was in, being alone in our home waiting for someone who was never coming back. I was going nuts and I looked at the door for weeks, wondering if she would change her mind and surprise me with her presence. I hoped she would. After a couple weeks I took Tim up on his offer and used one of my last free flights to go see him in Dallas.

Townsend

CHAPTER ELEVEN

The Alien Color Blue

It was July 3rd and I was very happy to see Tim. It was probably the first time I had smiled, or had anything to smile about, in a long time. He picked me up at the Dallas/Fort Worth Airport in a very familiar vehicle, the car we stomped around San Diego in years before. It helped having that anchor of familiarity. Tim immediately read the despair on my face like a past due expiration date. Curbside at DFW he jumped out of his car and gave me a big hug. His wife had waited at home to give Tim and I some alone time, predicting I may well be a huge mess. I was and when Tim hugged me, I felt like a pathetic failure. Tim was not wild on the idea of me marrying a flight attendant, pointing out they had a reputation for cheating and partying too much. He only mentioned it once, he was still my best man. We headed straight to the bar to get a drink before heading back to his house to unpack.

Tim lived in an area of Dallas called Oak Lawn and had a solid bar within walking distance- The Grapevine. Apparently, the Grapevine was a gay bar and Oak Lawn was the gayborhood, but that really didn't mean a thing to us. Tim's wife Lisa preferred to hang out with gay guys, so we often did also. Some of the craziest nights we had were with gay guys and their friends, the people we knew always had coke and bought our broke asses drinks all night long.

We had our first drink at The Grapevine at three in the afternoon when it was almost empty. We took our drinks to the rooftop patio to talk. We sat down at on iron patio furniture and sipped our beers. Tim ordered me two, so I was double-fisting, the bottles were already sweaty from the thick, humid summer heat.

"So, buddy… she's gone?" he asked in a soft tone.

"Yeah…" I sighed into my beer. "…I think so."

"What do you mean?" he asked.

Townsend

"Yea, she's gone but I think I can maybe get her back if I could just..."

"Stop," he interrupted.

"Look man, you've been married less than two years. She cheated on you once already. I kept my mouth shut but now this happened. So, I am not shutting up about it anymore," he said unequivocally.

My sips turned to chugs and I had just finished my first beer shortly after we sat down, partly because I was depressed and partly because Dallas was a sauna.

"You are twenty-nine. There is plenty of time to find the right girl. You have a big heart and you tried to make something work that made no sense. So move on," he continued.

"It's that fucking job, man! I think if I could convince her to choose me instead of..."

"She would have done it already," he interrupted.

WORLDLY

Tim was really giving me the tough love right out of the terminal gate.

"Women are thinkers, Jason. No doubt she has been thinking about this for a while. This was not an overnight decision. She chose the job over you," he said.

I sighed and chugged from the second beer. I was starting to get a buzz already from drinking so quickly, so I slammed the bottle a little hard onto the table.

"That fucking job..." I groaned looking up into the sky. Dark clouds were coming. I hadn't seen storm clouds like that in all my years living in San Diego. I had come to miss different kinds of weather and I looked forward to the thunderstorm coming in Dallas. That storm veered south and missed us but even the best weather person could not have predicted the hurricane on the horizon.

"... it's that damn job. It's not natural to be apart so much. It fuckin' killed us," I said.

I chugged from the second beer and tried to finish it with a bit too much left to go. I choked and spat a bit of beer on to the ground and proceeded to cough like a maniac.

Townsend

"There may have been *a little* more to it than her job, buddy," Tim muttered under his breath as he slapped me on the back and tried to get the rogue beer out of my lungs.

Back at Tim's house the pity party was ripe, Lisa was ready for me at the door with a beer in hand. I gladly accepted the beer and she showed me to the spare room. After I changed my T-shirt and jeans Lisa called me for dinner. Lisa had a killer guacamole, I mean seriously. I didn't even know I *liked* avocados until one of them made it once. The avocados were carefully picked for ripeness, diced and not fully mashed. It was spicy with cayenne, citrusy with both lemon and lime and had tiny dices of onion and jalapeno without the seeds. I have since tried to forge their recipe and cannot get it quite right. Lisa had my very own heaping bowl of the stuff to dunk my carne asada tacos into. One bowl of guacamole later I was starting to feel better, California comfort food.

"So, J... it's Friday. Are you feeling up to going out tonight?" she asked excitedly as we chomped away at our delicious tacos on the couch.

Tim and Lisa called me "J" for a nickname. I would always get it confused with "hey", answering pretty much anytime someone said it. It was OK though, they often teased my hearing. It was not the greatest from years of practicing drums and a couple years playing in a band, so the more I answered the more I could deny I was losing my hearing.

"Abso-fuckin-lutley!" I answered, keen on a night out and attempting to forget that I was about to be divorced.

"Fuck YEA! Just like the old days! The Three Fuck-it-eers!" Tim shouted with a full mouth and some lettuce fell out.

"Yea boyeee!" I shouted as I balanced my plate and leaned over to high-five Tim.

"Oh boys..." Lisa said sounding suddenly apprehensive but I think she was just kidding.

I tried to do the dishes, but Tim pushed me out of the way and told me I was fucking up his chore schedule and to go get ready to go out. I walked back in to the living room where Lisa was still finishing her plate.

"So, J... I was thinking (to avoid driving) we would walk down to The Grapevine. You saw it earlier...what do you think?" she asked.

Townsend

"Yea… sure. Whatever you guys wanna' do... it was pretty empty when we were there," I answered.

"Oh, that's because it was the afternoon, it won't be tonight. Here's the thing, it's not really a "gay bar" per se, but then it *kind of* is… is that OK?" she asked.

"*Yea*, sure. It's not my first gay bar," I responded.

"Good! Cuz I don't really know anywhere else to go…" she laughed.

"No worries."

"…and there are some *really* hot straight girls that go there," she finished and rose to give her plate to Tim for washing.

I did not really know how to process that information. I figured going to a gay bar was being more loyal to Maria. In the event we worked things out and she jealously asked what I did, I would tell her, in Dallas "I only went to a gay bar". I continued on to the spare bedroom, grabbed some fresh underwear and took a shower. Once back in the bedroom I tried on about everything I had in the suitcase before settling on the same Volkswagen "fahrvergnügen" T-shirt and jeans I was wearing before the shower. The idea of potentially talking to a real Texas belle was starting to make me nervous. I was very familiar with the act of going out to a bar, it was the new setting that was exciting.

Before long, we were back, and The Grapevine looked like a very different place. Before long we were at a very busy bar. People spilled out into the parking lot. The sound of people laughing and yelling amongst music could be heard a block away. As we approached the front door a grumpy bouncer looked at our identification and let us into the bar. He gave my California ID a closer inspection and examined it under a black light before letting me pass. We made our way through the main cavern of the bar, winding like Pacman through a maze of people and pool tables until we made our way outside to the patio where we got our drinks. Lisa got a vodka/soda and Tim, and I got two Shiner Bocks each. The bar was crowded, and we were not looking forward to returning for the next round.

We sat down at a wrought iron table with matching chairs under a patio roof and all lit cigarettes. Tim and Lisa smoked from the same pack of Turkish Gold's and I smoked

Townsend

Newports, a habit picked up at nineteen years old from my Crip wannabe friends in New York. Lisa hammered away at her cell phone while Tim quizzed me on Texas beers. I had initially resisted the Shiner believing it looked too dark for my liking but was very impressed by both its smooth taste and the fact that my friend knew I would like it.

"Oh! They're here!" Lisa shouted looking up from her phone.

"Oh yeah?" Tim responded and turned around with a grin to see.

Two men in their early thirties approached us from the entrance to the patio. Michael wore a nice pair of jeans with a light blue shirt tucked only in the front to show off a white leather belt. Andrew wore jeans, a black v-neck T-shirt and a ratty old Texas Longhorn's cap. Michael and Andrew immediately went for Lisa who looked overjoyed to see them. They eventually introduced themselves to me before sitting down and joining us.

"Hello… I'm Michael."

WORLDLY

"...and I'm Andrew," the other one said.

"Oh hi, I'm Jason."

Eight beers and three hours later I was a total of thirteen beers down for the day. After the rain stopped we all stumbled back to Andrew and Michael's house. I fell into a bush on the way and Tim found a ten-foot long pipe in a pile of garbage that he decided to sling over his shoulder and carry for about four blocks. Not one of us remember what he did with it and that thing was enormously heavy.

We drank some more, and I was quizzed on my upbringing, a story that Tim volunteered, and I was forced to elaborate on. Just as I began to feel like a freak Michael and Andrew sensed my apprehension and changed the subject. I do not remember much else of that night and the only evidence we had to go on were two blurry and drunken photographs I took on my cell phone. Even in my most inebriated state I always tried to photo-document life.

The next day I woke up on top of the bed and still wearing my "fahrvergnügen" T-shirt and jeans which reeked of alcohol being sweat out in the Texas summer heat. I woke to violent thunder clapping that sounded as if it were a block away. Heavy raindrops pounded on everything, satisfying an urge that was established in my childhood and neglected by my move to San Diego. I rolled over and smiled, happy that I was hearing rain, and happy that I had gone out the night before. I was beginning to feel human again, that even though my wife did not want me around, other people did. Even being a slight introvert, I feel alive around other people. I am a pack animal. I stumbled out to the kitchen and through to the deck where I found Tim and Lisa smoking.

"Hey guys. Could I bum one I can't find my pack," I said.

Tim reached in to his hoody pocket and threw me my pack of Newports.

"We found them up in the pole lamp in the living room. I turned the light on and there was this big rectangular shadow on the wall!" Tim laughed with Lisa, but they both cut it short as laughing worsened their headaches.

I must have mistaken the upside down shade of their pole lamp for a basketball hoop. I lit up a cigarette and we all sat in comfortable silence for a good five minutes while Tim rubbed Lisa's thigh and she showed him curtains on her cellphone. I glanced at them and pulled out my own cellphone to text Maria. I asked her if we could talk and that I just wanted to know if she was OK.

"Happy Fourth guys," I told my friends.

"Happy Fourth buddy," Tim responded.

"Well, we better get rid of these hangovers boys, we have to do it all again tonight," Lisa said, trying to scrape together some cheer.

"Yeah? What's the plan?" I asked Lisa.

"I had a text at ten A.M. from Michael asking us to meet them at The Grapevine again tonight. They are planning on a pub crawl."

"Awesome. I'm going to go throw up then," I said. The taste of the cigarette was turning my stomach. I put it out half-finished and ran to the bathroom where I hurled in to the toilet.

Unable to function, we ordered a pizza to the front door and Lisa gave us all a long evolved anti-hangover concoction

Townsend

of over-the-counter pills and vitamins. All three of us sat around and killed a few hours playing video games. In the last hour of video games Tim made Bloody Mary's and we started to come around. The rain continued to pound outside, and I almost did not care that it was the Fourth of July, I may have been just as happy spending it lying around with Tim and Lisa. My phone began to vibrate, something it had not been doing very often and I jumped to see who it was. It was Maria, so I sprung up from the couch and answered as I ran to the guest room and sat on the edge of the bed.

"H-hey, babe…" I answered sheepishly.

"Ugh, don't call me that. I am not going to talk to you if you call me that," Maria answered.

"I'm sorry. It's just force of habit."

"So, how are you?" she asked.

"I'm OK…"

"You're in Dallas?" she cut in.

"Y-yeah."

"Yes, I know. I saw your flight on my employee webpage," she told me.

"I-I just needed to get out of that apartment. Everywhere I look there is something that reminds me of you," I said.

I heard fireworks popping in the streets behind Maria.

"It's OK. Use them. Use them while you can. Fly every day, I don't care," she responded.

"How about if I fly to you? We can spend Fourth of July together," I said, throwing a Hail Mary.

In that moment I had figured out that she was in New York. The type of fireworks going off and the sounds of the streets I had all heard before.

"No, it's OK. You just have fun. Go do whatever you want to do, Jason," Maria told me.

I paused and sighed in silence, thinking of any magic combination of words I could put together to make her want to see me. I considered telling her I had brain cancer. I considered calling Alec to pick me up from JFK but realized she would see my flight. I considered simply telling her I loved her.

"Who's on the phone?" a deep male voice said in close range to Maria followed by the muffled sound of Maria trying to cover the microphone.

"I have to go, bye," Maria told me.

I stuttered trying to say anything but nothing of substance came out before the phone call was terminated, I was alone again sitting on the edge of the bed. A wave of hot anger came over me, washing from my toes up to my face, inflated pressure as if retained in my skull and I leapt up from the bed and smashed my cellphone to pieces on the wood floor. I stomped on the pieces until there were pieces of pieces. When the anger subsided, I was only left with deep, deflated sorrow. I left the room to find Tim, tears rolling down my face. Tim and Lisa turned around and gave me a look of shock as I entered the room. I spoke before they could think of what to say.

"I broke my phone."

WORLDLY

Tim and Lisa both lowered their gaze but made a face as if they understood what I was really saying.

Tim spoke in a calm and reassuring voice, "It's OK, buddy. You don't need a phone."

A short while later the three of us were again back at The Grapevine, this time arriving by cab. Again, standing out on the patio, the crowd was much bigger and there were no open patio chairs. Rain fell from the corners of the corrugated roofing as we sipped on beers trying to keep it down, our faces a little less cheerful than the night prior. We stood in comfortable silence sipping as we waited for Michael and Andrew. Our hangovers still had a grip on our heads and as for me, Maria had the rest.

I looked at a girl who sat alone, three empty chairs to herself. She looked beautiful to me, it may have been the lonely look in her eyes. Her sad look made me feel as if we were kindred, at least there in that moment. She stared down at the table and into her drink as if looking for something to appear from nothing. She seemed to not notice the raging crowd around her, her little empty table an oasis in chaos. Her glimmering brown hair parted and draped either side of her

Townsend

face where it came to rest on her blouse. I watched how the tips of her ears poked through her hair when a startling shock of almost alien blue appeared in a flash, when her gaze turned up through the crowd and caught mine. Embarrassed that I had been caught staring, I deflected her look and turned a few degrees away, leaving her only in my peripheral sight. I could only afford to admire her from afar.

Michael and Andrew soon pushed their way through the crowd from the entrance, greeting other familiar faces as they made their way to us. They smiled and took the time to hug all three of us. While hugging Andrew I gave in to temptation and looked back in the direction of the girl, who watched with a blank stare. I chugged my beer empty, feeling my nerves creeping in to get me.

"Hey bitches!" Andrew yelled, already intoxicated which really made me jealous.

"Let's go over here," Michael said.

"Hey, can we just get a couple beers first, I just finished this," I smiled and asked Michael.

"Sure…" he said as I pushed through to the bar.

I sat quietly waiting for the busy bartender to notice me. Moments later Michael smashed through the crowd, flirtatiously resting his forearm on a stranger sitting on a bar stool.

"Hey! Jerry! Eight Shiners!" he barked.

The bartender looked up immediately, smiled and nodded.

"Put 'em on my tab!"

"That's how you get that done. We are going to be at that table in the back, you see?" he said pointing to a crowded table that was really three tables pushed together.

"Yea!" I yelled over the music.

"Can you handle those beers by yourself?"

"Yeah sure! I'll make two trips!" I answered, actually glad to have some busy work.

Townsend

The bartender put down eight beers and I brought them to the table in two trips. Everyone in our immediate group took a beer, leaving four. I sat at the closer end at the head of the three-table group.

"Hey, who else are these for?" I asked Michael.

"You!" he shouted back, "Loosen the fuck up, Lurch!"

I looked back over in the direction of the girl, but my view was blocked. I leaned back in my wrought iron chair to peer around the obstruction and saw Andrew standing over her talking. Again, I was caught by a flash of alien blue eyes as she momentarily looked away from him and over to me. I flopped down in my chair, pale as a ghost. For the third time I had been caught staring like a looky-loo at car accident. The chair legs made a horrendous crashing sound against the concrete patio and Tim, who was sat to my right with Lisa, put a hand on my right arm.

"You OK, bud? Calm down," Tim inquired.

"Yeah. J, just play it cool alright?" Lisa said, with a thick layer of mischief in her voice.

"*He is so gonna' fuck this up*!" Lisa covertly laughed to Tim through her hand.

"What?" I asked, about sixty-percent sure I had understood her.

"Just play it cool, Goose," Tim said again with a calm and reassuring voice.

I listened to him. My crow's feet smoothed away, and my shoulders sank as I tried to relax, momentarily.

"Everyone! This is Grace! *Meet* Grace!" Andrew shouted from directly behind me.

I jumped like I had been shot in the ass but tried to add it to the natural motion of turning around to see Andrew. When I did, the girl with silky brown hair and alien blue eyes was with him. This time she looked over me and to the rest of the group sat at the table, giving a small shy wave.

"Hi," she quietly squeaked.

Townsend

"*Hi Grace!*" the table sang in drunken chorus, my voice a little louder as I was now trying to make her feel welcome and not so shy.

Andrew looked around for something.

"Hey, Jason… Jason this is Grace… go get Grace's chair before someone takes it, yea?" he asked.

I jumped up like a bumbling fool, and Tim smacked the bottom of his beer bottle into the top of mine causing it to foam uncontrollably. Half standing, I now was forced to quickly finish the rest of my beer that I had previously begun to nurse.

"You wa…ahem, you wanna' have my seat… Grace?" I asked.

"Sure… thank you," she replied as she looked into my eyes and gave me a polite smile. I briefly made eye contact with her but felt as if I was staring directly into the sun, so I looked away.

I scurried over to Grace's now-empty table that was being stripped of its chairs. Someone leaned in to grab the last

WORLDLY

chair, but I furiously swooped in and snatched it first and returned to our group, sitting at a somewhat awkward position behind Grace. Awkward enough that Tim reached in and pulled me closer, causing Grace to scoot over so I was now between Grace and Tim.

"How are you?" I smiled to Grace.

"I'm good! How are you?" Grace shouted over loud sound of Prince - 1999.

I actually thought about her question, and I hesitated a few seconds.

"Great!" I said nodding, with a shallow smile.

I handed Grace one of my three remaining Shiners and we clanked bottles. The following hour I spent trying, in almost meditative form, to push out thoughts of Grace and only think of my wife and what she may be doing. It was a very awkward hour spent almost avoiding Grace. In that hour Grace and I finished our beers in good timing as Michael and Andrew were calling everyone to get up and head to the next bar.

Townsend

"Hey, the rain stopped!" Grace shouted to me, trying to break the awkward silence.

"Yeah! Hey, you're my sunshine on a cloudy day!" the alcohol responded.

Her porcelain skin turned a bit red as she blushed and smiled at the clearly unexpected comment. On the way out, Tim said he had his card at the inside bar, which I could not recall him doing but was not about to question.

"Hey just meet us at the next bar!" Michael shouted to Tim.

Tim answered with a thumbs up, and I turned to see Andrew whispering into Grace's ear. Grace was dancing by herself a few paces away, and Andrew was quickly gone and out the door with Michael and the rest of the group. Grace stayed with us, awkwardly dancing with herself to a Morrissey song. Lisa slowly leaned in with an erect foot, and not so much kicked, but pushed me by my rectum over to Grace. This threw me not alongside her but basically on top of her. She did not object but instead put an arm around my shoulder as I began to dance with her. She kept her head down on my chest as we danced, somewhat drunkenly- and intimately. Before long the song was over, and she looked up at me, I again feeling the pain of looking into the sun, tried to look away but had nowhere else to look, so I just swallowed hard. She smiled, causing little dimples around her mouth and I almost panicked and farted. I however did not, and she pulled me by my hand to the wall by the front door as we continued to wait for Tim and Lisa. I held her hand as we mildly continued to dance.

"So, what do you do?" I asked.

Grace seemed a little annoyed as if she preferred the silence of the moment.

"I'm a dentist," she said quietly as if asking me not to pry any further.

"So, what... like you work for an office with other dentists?" I asked, guessing as she looked under thirty.

"No, I have my own practice." she said and leaned in again, resting her cheek on my chest.

Townsend

I then lost all interest in Grace, as I knew she was basically from another planet than me. She was beautiful and had graduated college, two qualities I previously had not been able to find at once in a girl who liked me back, except for my now estranged wife and that did not work out well.

"Well, I see you two have hit it off!" Lisa yelled from behind me and slapped me on the butt.

We quickly turned to find her and Tim ready to go and Grace let go of my hand.

The four of us left the bar and trotted down the streets of Oak Lawn to the next bar somewhere in Dallas. Tim and I were pretty drunk by now, Tim running ahead and doing "pirate pose" onto whatever horizontal surface he could find. I ran after him trying to knock the pirate on his ass. Lisa and Grace followed talking to each other. I pretended Grace and I had never held hands and danced. Tim pulled pirate pose on a bus stop bench and I knocked him into the wall of the bus stop, almost breaking the glass. Grace erupted in laughter, she was now coming out of her shell and not as shy. Still, I ignored her.

The next club much more fit the gay bar stereotype, filled mostly with men dancing to trance music. This lit Tim and I up, because we knew the music. We had been to three major raves in San Diego and one in Las Vegas. It took a bit of convincing as I previously was more in to heavy metal and punk, but trance grew on me. It has a steady, heavy beat that speaks a universal language and the synthesizers offer a calm that I did not see in metal. I was surprised to hear the music at all in the state of Texas.

"Fuck yeah! Markus Schultz!" Tim excitedly yelled to me as we walked right in the dance club.

"Fuck yeah!"

After the straight men were done yelling about dance music, Michael ran up to greet us.

"You boys better stay close to your women in here!" he yelled.

Andrew ran up with a round of drinks all ready for us. That blew my mind out of my ears. These guys thought ahead to buy us drinks, so we had them when we walked in the bar. I have never once had a straight buddy run up to me when I

Townsend

got to a bar and hand me a drink. Something about that made me feel extremely welcome, like I was home. Grace swooped in from behind and grabbed me by the hand. She pulled me onto a crowded dance floor. Wanting to give off the "straight vibe" I held her close and she turned her back to grind on me. I put my nose in to her fragrant silky brown hair- and surrendered to Dallas. I was beginning to really like it there.

The next thing I remember is getting out of a cab in front of Lisa and Tim's house, Grace sat between them in the back seat. Lisa grabbed the keys out of Tim's hand as she came without a purse, Tim kept their ID's and keys.

"We have to pee!" she yelled as they stumbled and rushed out of the cab.

I stared out of the window and watched in terror as Lisa put an arm around Grace and they disappeared into the house.

Tim paid the cabby and I sat on the porch stoop, Tim joining me.

"What do I do?" I asked my best friend.

"What do you mean?" he asked in a sort of coy tone.

"Whatya mean 'what do I mean'? What do I do? Grace is *amazing...* but she is also way out of my fucking league," I whined.

"Dude," he started.

"I mean, what now? I go in there and play an awkward tug of war with my brain between Maria and trying to make a move on a girl that terrifies me?" I rambled on.

"Dude... don't worry about it. Maria is fucking someone else tonight. Alright?" he slurred.

I looked angry at him but quickly lost my understanding as to why, because he was probably right.

"Look, she left you. From everything you said it sounds like she is done. So, there's no pressure, just enjoy your time in Dallas. Have a rebound. You'll feel better," he said.

"I-I have never had a one-night-stand, man. I don't do that... like...fundamentally," I complained. "I hook up with girls I like, so it has always been more than once."

Townsend

"Stop overthinking. You overthink everything, it's your downfall. Do you like her?" he asked.

"Do I *like* her? *Of course,* I like her! Have you *seen* her? Have you *met* her? She's *fucking amazing*!" I yelled back drunkenly. "She's like... finding diamond-crusted gold in a shit-swamp!"

"Then she meets your criteria! Get up there!" Tim said, getting up and stamping his cigarette into the stoop.

On the walk inside, I thought about what I would say. I obsessed over what I would say that would not come out sounding creepy or weird. We ran into Lisa in the living room.

"Grace went to sleep," she said.

My heart clanked around in the bottom of a bucket.

"She's asleep in the spare room," she continued.

"Oh, should I sleep on the couch then?" I asked.

"I... dunno. Maybe you should ask her," She answered facetiously.

"Well I'll just go get some pajamas," I answered.

Five minutes after being home and Grace was fast asleep in my bed? Something seemed not right.

"Go get her, buddy. Hey… if… if she *wants* to be got. Got that?" Tim asked.

"Dude she's drunk, what if she doesn't want… no I better sleep on the couch," I argued.

Tim shoved me, and I continued to the room to check on Grace and see about some pajamas. I carefully opened the bedroom door and Grace lay facing away from me, quiet as a mouse under the covers. I could not make out much but a silhouette. I stumbled, tripping over the mess of clothes I had made before leaving that night. I bent over and dug through the mess looking for shorts and a fresh T-shirt. Shortly after that Grace let out a little groan and she turned in my direction.

"Hey, will you cuddle with me?" she asked.

"Yep!"

Townsend

I pulled off my shirt and stood next to the bed thinking of what to do with my jeans. I decided to leave them on and jumped into the bed and wrapped my arms around Grace. She did not quite turn to me but turned her face to the ceiling.

"So, I'm your sunshine on a cloudy day, huh?" she asked.

"You have no idea." I answered.

I leaned in and kissed Grace, she inhaled deeply as if she had been waiting a whole year to be kissed, and maybe she had. She put her hand behind my head and I put one of mine behind her jaw. I put my bottom lip between hers and she kissed it. I put her full, juicy bottom lip in my mouth and before long she pulled at the back of my thigh.

"Can you take your pants off?" she asked, stopping for a moment.

I left the bed to remove my pants, taking a moment to clear my brain and focus on one thing, and one thing alone. When I got back in the bed I crawled between her legs and worked my way up to her like a lion stalking prey. She slapped her arms around me and drug her nails up my back. Before long we realized that the old metal bedframe (an antique of Lisa's) was not held together very well. It made loud spring sounds and smashed against the wall. Grace was not shy or quiet anymore and I worried the noise was too much for Tim and Lisa. So, I pulled Grace from the bed and bent her over it instead. We moved from the bed to the floor, where we would eventually pass out for the remainder of the night with big, happy smiles; Grace laying on my chest and I on a blanket on the floor.

When I woke in the morning I was on the floor alone, no blue-eyed, stellar remnant on top of me, but I still felt her gravity. I barely pulled on basketball shorts before running out of the room. I found Lisa in the kitchen making herself some coffee in a Keurig.

"Coffee?" she asked.

"Did Grace… she left?" I asked impatiently.

"She just left, she hung around all morning. It's eleven, boy," she answered.

"*Shit!*"

Townsend

"She left her phone number for me to give to you, don't worry," she said. "She knows you don't have a phone."

"Aww shit, why does she know *that*?"

"I told her… so what? Oh, and she came out of the room this morning with the keypad stuck to her butt. So that kind of gave it away."

She took a step towards me.

"Chill out, J! It's all good!" she finished and handed me her cup of coffee. "Here take this I'll make another one."

Lisa and I retreated to the couch where we slumped down together. I could not shake the disappointment that Grace was gone. It felt like I needed to see her sober for confirmation that it really happened and that she really matched the memory in my brain. I just wanted to see those eyes in the morning.

"So, do you want to know what she said?" Lisa asked me, breaking the silence and dragging me out of my own head.

"Yeah!" I shouted a little too loud.

Lisa paused and sipped her coffee, letting me brew a moment.

"She said that she wasn't... expecting *you*."

"What... expecting? What does that mean... is that good?" I asked but could not keep back my cheesy smile. I broke into a chuckle.

"Yeah of course, J. It's good," she answered.

Lisa's phone vibrated, she snatched it up and squinted at the screen. It vibrated again, and I realized it was a phone call. Lisa answered it.

"Hello?... Oh no!" she said into her phone. "Oh shit, where are you? OK, Jason is coming to get you. OK, bye."

Lisa hung up and I shot her my most confused face.

"She has a flat tire. This is for you, kid. Take Tim's Pontiac."

I ran to the bedroom with the urgency of a firefighter leaving for a call. I pulled on my jeans and closest T-shirt I

Townsend

could find. I skidded out to the living room and pulled my sneakers on without socks. Lisa handed me a piece of paper.

"Those are directions for how to get there. She is in the Walmart parking lot. She said she is right out front; you can't miss her."

"What kind of car does she have?" I asked.

"I don't know... I'll text her and tell her to stand outside her car. Go!" she yelled at me.

I flumped out of the front door and ran to Tim's car, I jiggled the key in the driver's door as I had known to do when it lived in San Diego, and I took off squinting at the piece of paper. A few questionable turns later I found Walmart and Grace. I found Grace almost before the Walmart sign, I realized then I could pick her out of a stadium. I skid to a halt behind her SUV and jumped out, suddenly, feeling an awkward fog between us. I pranced up to Grace, leaned her against her SUV and French-kissed her.

"Goodbye." I said afterwards.

"Yeah, you know… I didn't know if you wanted me around, today," she said, now returning to her shy demeanor and dimpled smile.

I snorted.

"Uh, yeah. Yeah, I… I was sad when I saw you were gone," I told her.

Grace slapped her hands to her sides.

"Well, do you know how to change a tire? I'll come back for a few hours."

"Of course, I can change a tire."

This brought a big cheesy grin to her face and I wondered why she was surprised. I changed her tire in about twenty minutes and since I was now lost, I followed her back to Tim's house.

I spent that last full day in Dallas spending as much time with Grace as I could. The four of us lay around and played video games, Lisa beating most of us most of the time. Grace's few hours turned into about six, but eventually she

Townsend

really did have to be headed home as we all had work the following day. I walked her out to her car, the sun still up but falling in a clear blue sky.

"You really were my sunshine on a cloudy day, Grace," I told her as I kissed her goodbye, not knowing if I would see her again.

CHAPTER TWELVE

Sunshine Over San Diego

Back in San Diego my mind was reeling. Walking into my apartment, reality had crashed back in. My Christian upbringing was tugging me at one arm and my heart tugging at the other. I felt I had gravely sinned, no matter what my wife may have been doing on Fourth of July. I felt almost bipolar, a million times happier then when I had last seen that apartment and a million times more in trouble. Regardless, the first thing I did was dig through my junk drawer to find an old cellphone and pop my SIM card in that I had salvaged from the wreckage of my last cellphone. I plugged the phone in and it burst to life, as a few missed messages from a 214-area code came through.

Hi, Jason. I just wanted

Townsend

to say I had a great time

with you and I am glad I

stuck around. – Grace

A smile came over my face and along with a deep feeling of relief. I sent her a message back asking if I could call her. Over the next two weeks I worked more than usual and swung my hammer harder. I already knew what I would do, even if no one else did. Over that time, I also spoke to Grace every day, sometimes for hours. Not an hour went by without my phone alerting me to a message from Grace. I told her all about my life and my recent marriage problems, and she told me about her life and recent ex-fiancé, an oral surgeon who could neither change a tire or keep his dick in his pants. Eventually my wife called to tell me she was coming to get her things. This put some question between Grace and me. She told me to just be honest about whatever happened when Maria was in town.

The day Maria arrived I picked her up at the airport and had what would probably be the most awkward car ride of my life, filled with generic and polite questions from both sides. Once at the apartment the questions became more specific.

"I am going to stay one night. I'll pack tonight and call movers tomorrow to move my boxes to storage. I'll sleep on the couch. You know, I called you later that night...why didn't you answer?"

"I broke it… after you hung up on me." I sighed.

"You broke it? Why are you such an asshole, Jason?"

"You know, it's pretty frustrating to not know where your wife is or how to fix a broken marriage." I answered.

"I thought maybe you were with someone," she muttered.

"Were you?" I laughed.

"You know what? I know you didn't, but I wish to God you would have just fucked someone else, Jason. This is over. Maybe that would bring you some closure and you would let me go."

Townsend

I laughed to myself a bit and all my questions as to whether I had done the right thing faded.

"OK," I answered. "Look, you don't need to get a truck. I'll move the stuff for you tomorrow and take you to the airport. There is no reason we can't be decent to each other at least, is there?" I said.

Maria thought for a moment and looked at me trying to feel out if I was trapping her. I raised my eyebrows and slapped my hands to my sides.

"Yea. Alright. I could use saving the money, this whole thing is killing my bank account," she said.

I stared at her and scoffed.

"Yea, that really sucks for you," I said, and she missed the sarcasm as English was her second language.

"Yes, it does, Jason. Thank you for acknowledging that. You know this isn't all fun and games," she replied.

"You can have the bedroom. I'll sleep on the couch," I told her.

WORLDLY

With another surprised look she took me up on it and packed her things in to the plastic crates we had previously used to move in. I lay on the couch and sent a few text messages to Grace, including a picture of me lying alone on my couch as per her request.

The next day I used my dolly to haul Maria's crates out to my '91 Ford Bronco. Once everything was loaded that she wanted to save, we went to the storage unit that we had rented to store my work tools. I switched the tools for her crates and gave her the key.

"You don't need the storage unit?" she asked.

"Nope," I responded as I pulled the dolly loaded with my tools and checked my phone. Maria peered over to see who I was texting, and I pulled away.

"What? You care who I'm texting?" I asked.

"N-no," she said hesitantly. Gears were starting to turn.

Once back at my apartment I decided to call Grace, so I told Maria I would be right in. I caught Maria looking back curiously as I placed the phone call.

Townsend

"I'm sorry it's driving me nuts that she's there with you. I wasn't going to say anything," Grace said.

"Oh, don't worry. She'll be gone in a few hours."

"Did anything happen between you two? Just tell me, she *is* your wife," she asked.

"No… I promise. I slept on the couch. That was it."

"I can't take this anymore. I don't know how long I can wait and not know what is going to happen."

"Well, I was thinking. There's not a lot holding me in San Diego and Tim and Lisa offered me their spare room for a while…"

Grace paused and was silent for a bit.

"Are you serious?" she asked quickly.

"Yeah. Why not?"

Grace screamed. I did not know why she was so excited. The last I saw her I basically ran away from her all night, but we did build a strong connection over the phone during the weeks that followed. Grace tested my loyalty by dragging her feet ending the conversation, and I did not rush her. I wanted her to feel my loyalty was to her. I told Grace I would call her after I dropped Maria at the airport and returned to the apartment.

"So, I was thinking, the lease is good for another few months, why don't you just keep the apartment?" Maria graced me as I entered the apartment.

"No, I think we should just terminate it," I answered coldly.

"Why? What's going on with you?"

"I'm moving to Texas," I said, my heart jumped saying it out loud, which was the first moment I realized I was really going to do it. I must have been crazy.

"*What*? Why?" Maria exclaimed.

"Do you want a divorce?" I asked.

"Yes."

Townsend

"Then it's none of your business."

Maria slumped off and grabbed her bags. I took her largest suitcase and loaded it into the Bronco. The ride to the airport was silent, but I could feel Maria's gears turning. Once at the airport I unloaded Maria's bags and handed them to her, a wave of solemn depression hit me like a baseball bat in the gut. Maria leaned in to give me a hug; reluctantly I gave in and hugged her back, and she held on for a long time.

"Are you going to be OK?" she asked.

"I think so..." I said.

We looked at each other one last time, and then I drove away, dropping my flight attendant wife at the airport one final time.

In one week I sold everything left in that apartment. The trick to selling a house full of crap is not to list everything individually. List everything as one big estate sale. Vultures will flock to you and pick your bones clean in no time. Someone else will pay to rid you of your marriage spoils. By the end of the week I felt much lighter and my wallet was fatter. At least fat enough to pay for the gas to Texas and live for a short while. I had a couple of job interviews lined up for when I arrived which meant I was now on a schedule.

Over the remainder of the week I said goodbye to my friends; again, an optimal way to do things is quickly. Drag it out longer and saying goodbye will become exponentially harder. The day I loaded up was an exciting day. I felt like a new future was ahead of me, again. There was not a lot to load, mostly tools. Never sell your tools, they will make you money wherever you are. They are a great investment if you can use them, but do not hold a good resale value. I left sunny San Diego on a Friday.

Townsend

CHAPTER THIRTEEN

<u>Texan</u>

In this current tectonic arrangement, the drive from San Diego to Dallas is roughly 1,300 miles and takes twenty hours to complete. As I have always been the "just do it" type of person, I decided to drive it in one straight shot. After-all, several years ago I made the drive from New York to San Diego, so I had experience. I left extremely late, having messed around with truck maintenance and making sure my load was secure and valuables hidden. My '91 Bronco had a soft top on the back and as I started out, I decided to leave it off. I headed down the 8 East off into the desert, top down and without a frown. I just prayed that both I and my Bronco would survive the twenty-hour trip, but we were both built like tanks- or so I thought.

WORLDLY

The drive to New Mexico was brutal. By the time I had reached Albuquerque the buzz of excitement had worn off and I was now tired. I had stopped for gas once already and bought a couple of energy drinks to help me keep going. It may not have been the best idea to leave at ten at night, as I was tired from the start, but I am by no means a stranger to doing dumb shit. I remember an increased presence of police cars, their coloring not as threatening as in other states, and wondered if they were out for the real Walter White. I had no time to stop and see landmarks from my favorite television show, Grace was waiting. New Mexico was passed in a blink of an eye; you can drive through it even before you get bored of being there.

Before long I was celebrating, as I had passed into Texas. Grace called to congratulate me, but also to warn that storms were on the horizon. She had been watching the weather and warned me that I was driving head on into a nasty one, and that I might just want to get a hotel and let it pass. I was two energy drinks in and feeling strong, so I told her I would brave the storm and plow ahead, after all, I thought I was close. Texas is such an enormous state that when I thought I was close I was only a little over half way there. I was getting very sick of seeing desert and just wanted to be at Tim's house. I

Townsend

entered Texas somewhere around El Paso and so I put my head down and kept on chugging.

About a quarter of the way into Texas, out in the middle of flat nowhere, I had begun to enter the storm. I was driving into the wind and being pelted. The Bronco's roof was solid over the driver but removable over the back. My top was down. As I was driving into the wind I found if I maintained a speed of forty-five miles per hour the rain would ride the slip-stream right over my tools and suitcase, but I could not stop. I was being pounded by rain which woke me up a bit, and that was good, but I was also running out of gas, which was very bad. If I stopped for a few moments my power tools would be soaked. Out in the Texas desert there are not options for gas stations every few miles, so when I saw one, I stopped. I drove as fast as I could off the exit and down the little access road to the station. Once there I found that the carport was almost totally filled with other travelers escaping the pelting rain. They were just camped out, in their fully-covered vehicles waiting it out. Luckily the sight of my dumb ass inspired someone to make room for me. An old man moved his car to the middle pass between two sets of pumps letting me have a pump and shelter. The looks I got out in the Texas desert that night I have tried to forget. I arrived at the gas station driving a turquoise Bronco in the middle of a horrendous thunder storm with the soft top removed. I am sure my California license plates explained it all. I filled up on gas, relieved that I would not run dry without half a roof in the middle of a huge storm. I considered putting my top on but there was a problem. The top took over an hour to put on with over a hundred snaps and I am both impatient by nature and I was losing steam. This was now a donkey/carrot situation and the carrot was a warm, dry bed. I called Grace who sounded apprehensive about the lunacy of which I informed her, so we decided it best that I just press on and I'd call her when I got to Dallas. Grace had been up the same amount of time I had, trying to co-pilot from Dallas and keep me company from afar, but she was exhausted and needed a nap. So, after filling up and buying two more large energy drinks I decided to do something no one else under that carport did.

The rain was flopping out of the sky, drops so big they could be mistaken for hail when they hit the ground (big ol' fat rain, Forest). I decided to look twice as insane as I did when I arrived, and head off back in to the storm, loaded with cargo, without securing my soft top. Huge bolts of lightning lit up the interior of the truck brighter than daylight. Thunder

Townsend

clapped and, for a while, I did not even have to open an energy drink, fear for my life did the job of keeping me awake nicely. I sped at fifty miles an hour, the absolute fastest I could go before my big heavy SUV started to hydroplane. This made a strong enough slip-stream that kept my tools dry, and after about an hour, I passed through the storm like passing through a shower curtain. All of a sudden I could see, and the air was clear and muggy again, yet I could turn around and see the hazy atmosphere that contained a thunder storm.

After passing through the storm and the danger was over, exhaustion set in. There was no longer anything keeping me awake. I was about to the middle of Texas and now heading north to Dallas, but my eyes were heavy. I slammed another energy drink, straight down the hatch and put on the heaviest metal I could find. In the final few hours the battle was against myself, I was four energy drinks in and was both exhausted and jittery.

I felt my heart doing weird things and I was starting to panic. I was now so tired that it was hard to lift my arms, the steering wheel was propping them up, and the population was becoming denser. I entered through Fort Worth feeling I had only minutes to either get there or die of a heart attack. So, on the edge of Fort Worth I bought another energy drink. The drinks were now giving me minutes instead of hours. By the time I entered Dallas I was having an all-out panic attack. I had gotten them since I was a child, but this was by far the worst as it was burning off fuel from five large energy drinks in a single day. I had to pull over.

The traffic was now heavier and almost impossible to safely navigate during the height of both exhaustion and a panic attack. Not wanting to scare Grace, I called Lisa. Lisa talked me off a ledge and told me I was only ten minutes away, ten minutes from a warm bed. She waved the carrot. She said all I had to do was throw my Bronco in the driveway and run into the house, that she would park it in the garage, so my things would not be stolen. If I tried to park in a residential garage in the state I was in, it would be demolition, and there sure as hell was no energy to unload. Lisa's calm and rational words served as enough inspiration, and I completed the last ten minutes. I drove 1,300 miles in twenty hours, all in one shot. I got there and flopped out of the driver's door, running up to Lisa in an exhausted panic and hyperventilating. She was waiting for me in the driveway with a hug and a tall glass of tequila.

Townsend

"Oh... my God... I think I... am going to die." I told her, breathing heavy.

I panted trying to get the words out, panicking like a cheetah was after me. She gave me another big hug and rubbed my back until I calmed slightly.

"No, you won't, you made it, you're here. Drink this straight down, you'll feel better," she said.

I did, and I felt my heart slow and the panic become duller instead of like the sharp jabs of a knife.

"Go, go sleep. You need it," Lisa told me.

I hugged her again and thanked her as I ran into the house from the back yard. I entered through the kitchen where Grace stood against the counter. I had not expected her to be there and she served again as pure sunshine on my dark and cloudy day. I hugged her and kissed her as if I had just returned from war and she undressed me and helped me to bed. She put her small hand on my heart and felt it beating through my chest and it slowly begin to calm. I asked her if she would scratch my back, but she asked to stay in the position we were in.

WORLDLY

Panic attack or not, I slept like I had never slept before. I passed out so deep I was not sure I would awaken from it, like my heart might just fall asleep also. Luckily, I did wake up the next morning and the first thing I saw was my own nose, buried in Grace's silky brown hair. At that moment, I had won and could not be happier. My life had just started again and I was excited to follow it. Grace drooled through her night-guard onto my chest and as crazy as it sounds, I began to love her.

Grace became a fixture in our house. By my second week in Dallas I had gotten a job as a foreman for a remodeling company and the future was looking bright. Almost immediately I started spending time at Grace's house and she put me on projects that had needed to be done for some time. I hung pictures and fixed other little things around the house that were a big problem to her and easy for me. I spent time meeting her friends and trying to expand my group in Dallas. I spent nearly every free moment with Grace, and very little time at home with Tim and Lisa.

Grace and I were in that honeymoon stage when you want to spend every waking moment either with, or conversing with, the other person. This started to bring tension

Townsend

with Tim and Lisa for although I was paying rent for the room, I was rarely there. Looking back now I can see how they were annoyed with the situation. They gave me a room to rent and I immediately spent all my time with Grace, basically only coming home to change.

Lisa and Tim were planning their wedding and I had the honor of being best man. It was even difficult getting me to show up for the tux fitting between work and Grace expecting me to be with her all the time. It did not take long for the monotony of work and schedule to take over, but there were big things to look forward to. Tim and Lisa decided to have a joint bachelor and bachelorette party in Las Vegas and the group including Grace and I were all flying to join in. We were all going to see Tim, Lisa and my favorite trance DJ's, *Above and Beyond*. As the best man, and Tim's best friend, I had a heavy responsibility to him that weekend.

CHAPTER FOURTEEN

The Bachelor/Bachelorette Party

I had to work the latest that day, so my flight was the last to arrive. Grace went ahead with everyone else. I had been trying to call Grace since I landed. She picked up once, it was loud and then the call disconnected. This situation felt familiar and reminded me of another phone call I had the night I met Grace. The whole trek to find the group I was trying to keep my mind out of the gutter and trust that everything was fine, after all, Grace knew what I had just been through with Maria only a couple months before.

By the time I arrived everyone was already drunk, a rare occasion that I was sober when everyone else was not. When I finally found the group, I found them loud and rowdy with conspiracy theories ready for me. Apparently, Grace had run off with three strange men shortly after their group arrived.

Townsend

This was probably the worst news I could have imagined at the time. For three hours I tried to rationalize the situation and hope for the best, calling Grace's dead phone about every fifteen minutes. This put a bit of a damper on my time with Tim and I am sure I have been more fun to be around. Finally, Grace sent me a text message in broken English telling me she was drunk and asked me to come get her. She was at a different casino and I pretty much sprinted the whole way there.

When I finally found her, she was with three men I did not recognize, they looked about our age or slightly older. Grace was sloppy drunk, leaning on one of them, and as I approached my blood pressure started to spike. When she saw me, she ran up and jumped on me, planting a big kiss on me that tasted like vodka. She introduced the three guys as friends from Dallas. She had known them almost all her life, they were friends of her older sister. Two of them were married and the one who was not was there for his bachelor party. This made me feel roughly eighty-percent better about the circumstances.

Grace wanted to have dinner with them and I hesitantly agreed as we had a group of our own waiting for us.

Regardless, I figured Grace could use water and something in her stomach, so I tried my best to politely hurry the meal. On the way back, I asked Grace if she thought it was a little rude to disappear like that, but she deflected any blame, saying that she felt out of place in our group without me there. I was just glad to have her back and was ready to finally begin the bachelor party with my best friend.

As I had feared our lengthy disappearance had not left us in good graces with our group. Grace's immediate departure put a rift in our group. Lisa was not very happy to see Grace when I returned with her. Regardless, there was not much time to worry about it as we all had to split up and get ready for the *Above and Beyond* show. The girls went to their room and the boys went to theirs. I apologized to Tim that we took so long getting back and the issue was resolved by the end of the sentence. The male group was finished and ready to leave long before the girls were, so Tim was shoving booze in my face, encouraging me to catch up with everyone else. I of course was glad to, and finally felt relief as if the vacation had now just begun and I could finally relax.

We drank and horsed around until there was a knock at the door. It was Grace, asking for me and she did not look

Townsend

happy. She said that the other girls were not making her feel welcome and that they were all giving her the cold shoulder, so she was going to leave. Now having a bit of alcohol in my system I quickly reacted and set out down the hallway to find Lisa, hoping to resolve the issue. Grace resisted and insisted on leaving but I was not hearing it, telling her it would be fine and just let me talk to her. Lisa came out and was indeed very defensive with me, upset that Grace had disappeared with three guys when we were all supposed to be part of a bachelor/bachelorette party. Grace overheard the discussion and was getting madder by the minute and closer to the elevator.

"You know what? We also do not like feeling that we aren't good enough to hang out with her if you are not here. Technically since she is a girl she is my guest. Tell her just apologize and don't disappear again and everything will be fine," Lisa said.

This drove Grace to the edge. The audacity that someone would ask her to apologize was too much and she was now high-tailing it to the bank of elevators.

WORLDLY

"You're crazy Lisa! I don't need this drama!" Grace yelled as she stomped away, and I started to question the true source of the 'drama'.

I let out a frustrated groan as I realized it was not yet time for me to relax. I ran after Grace and caught her by the elevator. What happened next, I will only paraphrase because the remembrance of it is too irritatingly pathetic to endure dwelling on.

For a pain-staking hour I begged and pled with Grace to stay with our group. I had to carefully choose my words, having backtracked from accusations that this is ruining my best-man experience as this only infuriated her further. Thirty minutes into the begging, the group left us behind and I took Grace to the boy's room to plead in private. Grace would not budge, and after an hour of begging told me she was leaving and to let her go, that she was going to stay with her three friends from Dallas.

This crushed me, in a way that it took almost another hour for me to get enough of a grip on myself to leave and join the rest of my party. To do what I came there to do.

Townsend

Once at the *Above and Beyond* show I stood in the hall outside the club. The walls were glass and I could clearly see in. I could see our group about twenty feet away dancing and I started to call Tim on the phone. One of my favorite songs came on and I began to serial dial Tim to come out and make sure everything was OK with us before going in.

I saw Tim pull out his illuminated phone and lean in to say something to Lisa before returning his phone to his pocket. For some reason, perhaps it was the alcohol, I thought it best to leave Tim to cool off. I thought my presence would further the problem and take away from his bachelor party. So, I decided to abandon the idea of seeing a show I had looked forward to, gave away my eighty-dollar ticket to someone outside, and went back to the boy's hotel room to wait for Tim. I curled up in pain, lying in the double bed closest to the window and waiting for hours unable to sleep. Finally, I heard a keycard open the hotel door. Instead of four guys, only Tim and Lisa entered the room.

"Hey…" I told them.

No one answered me.

WORLDLY

"Hey, Grace left. I went to the show, but I didn't know if you guys even wanted me there."

"We didn't, J," Lisa answered for Tim.

Lisa helped Tim pack his clothes into a duffle bag and kept him focused on doing it quickly.

"Guys, I'm sorry. Look, I didn't know what to do. Grace left me to go hang out with those dudes. Can't we just forget about her? Do I have to lose everyone this weekend?" I again found myself pleading.

The door closed behind Tim and Lisa and I drunkenly sobbed myself to sleep. Bright and early the next morning Grace called, sober with a softer disposition. She asked how I spent my night and was further infuriated with Tim and Lisa. At this point I began to wonder if she had a point. I accepted her offer to go get our own suite and have our own vacation. I took a cab back to the same casino I had retrieved her from the night before.

I ate breakfast with her and her three friends. We had a good time and I got along with her friends, who all went out of their way to feel sorry for me. They even insisted on buying

Townsend

my breakfast. Afterwards they left, and Grace and I went to the front desk to get the best room we could find. Grace got a room with a hot tub, kitchenette and floor-to-ceiling windows. The sex that night was rough. I pinned her up against the windows and fucked her as we looked out at Las Vegas. I wondered where my people were and what they were doing as I looked out that window. Grace filled the hot tub with bubbles and after yet another round we retired to bed. For a while longer she rubbed my chest from her favorite position in bed, and we talked about the future before falling asleep.

We checked out shortly before noon the next day and took a cab to the airport. My flight left an hour after Grace's, so I walked her to her gate. We both felt we had saved a piece of the weekend the night before, although there remained an ten-ton elephant in the room.

We sat waiting for her flight to board and she rested her head on my shoulder as I played with my phone. I felt her head dart up and I looked up to see what she was seeing. What she saw was a shocked Lisa and friends, pointing and chattering about us as if they had just seen the Manson Family. They stared for a moment until they were gone, continued off down the hall to their gate.

WORLDLY

I was the first to arrive back home at Tim and Lisa's and waited for them on the porch. Lisa said hello almost as though nothing was wrong and continued on inside with her bag, leaving Tim and I to duke it out on the porch. By this point I was livid. I'd had over twenty-four hours to dwell on the incident and had only discussed it with Grace. I had decided that Tim had acted unfairly. I was very upset because we could never get that bachelor party back, it was gone. Tim had the chance to recognize that I was there after Grace had run off but chose to push his best man away. I had a few good zingers ready to hit him with and after he heard them, he simply agreed and apologized. He said that we could have our own night out to make up for it. He said that due to being ridiculously drunk he and Lisa had overreacted towards me. Just like that it was over, for Tim and me.

Grace however, was another story. Lisa retained her wish for an apology for her to be invited to the wedding. I very much wanted Grace to be my date. The ordeal stretched for over a month, with several conversations between us about when an apology might possibly occur. Also, on several touchier occasions I tried to coerce Grace in to apologizing to Lisa. I succeeded and showed up at the house with Grace for the first time since Vegas. When Grace walked in Lisa had apparently walked past her and not said "hello" or acknowledged her presence, so Grace stormed out of the house and the issue remained unresolved.

Tim sided with Lisa and I reluctantly sided with Grace. When I spoke to them about it on the phone I harshly blamed Lisa because Grace was sitting next to me. Grace and Lisa never made up, and not only was I not the best man, but I did not even attend their wedding. Later that day I went back to get my things and I never saw my two favorite friends again.

CHAPTER FIFTEEN

Praying for Grace

There was little time to dwell on regret about the situation. Out of necessity I moved in with Grace the day I left Tim and Lisa's. We had been dating less than six months. I felt as if I was suddenly Grace's problem and worried if I had moved in too soon. We did our best not to think about it and kept busy. The fact always remained in the back of my mind: I was alone in Texas and the only friend I had was my girlfriend. The fresh excitement of moving in together kept things interesting, even grocery shopping together was fun. Grace did not keep a constant social life. Instead she would go through spurts of being very socially active at bars and clubs until she burned out and suddenly became a homebody-health-nut. When we met she had just decided to start going out again and it was game-on. It did not take long for me to understand why she would burn out.

Townsend

The first night that I met her sister and brother-in-law was at the Policeman's Ball in downtown Dallas. The pair looked as if they were chiseled out of marble, her sister Abigail's fake breasts stood out far enough to rest a beer on. They were popular modern people- they modeled, did soft-core porn and had met at a swinger's party. Her husband Nick had played professional football at some point and looked like someone who could have played Jesus (the healthy version) if he only had a beard.

I still have no idea why we were at the Policeman's Ball; it may have been a dare they were making good on. They did not seem the type that would ever turn down a dare. I felt extremely out of place from the get-go. I was dressed in a suit and tie and surrounded by cops, who surely would not be happy with my presence if they knew I had once upon a time socked one of their New York co-workers in the face.

Not long after getting drinks and making introductions Nick asked me to follow him to the bathroom where he handed me a bag of coke and a car key. Memories of New York flooded back, but this was clearly a different animal, so I went for it. I horked a fat bump of coke just before a cop came in to take a leak. I had just understood why Nick handed me a single key to do the bump, a single key does not jangle. I wiped my nose and made sure to save any residual sniffing once outside of the bathroom. I washed my hands and once outside Nick greeted me with wide eyes and a baffled grin, I greeted him with a huge sniff. All four of us ran around sorting cocaine right under the noses of authority all night long and drinking.

We made up varying stories of who we were to strangers that would try to talk to us. Abigail attracted a lot of attention, Nick being present or not. Nick seemed the type of guy that did not know the definition of jealousy. If some guy came up to hit on his wife, he would act as if he'd just made a new friend. The guy had great stories about everything, but unlike most story-tellers, he was not a one-upper. He asked more questions then he gave statements in a conversation, and he seemed interested in the answers. Nick seemed to be role-model material, I wanted to be more like him, Grace wanted me to also. She really did say that to me often, "you should be more like Nick, he would _____". I think Grace would have rather been with her brother-in-law

Later that night when we were all snowed out and starting to get rowdy Nick and I decided it best to leave the

Townsend

company of members of the police department. They had rented a room in the same hotel as the ball and they'd had the foresight to get two beds. I was happy to get Grace away from prying eyes because she looked great and was getting obnoxious. Two great reasons to not be around male cops. Once she started blowing lines, her appetite grew exponentially, and it was time to get her somewhere safe.

We all went up to the room where the coke dealer (who was a real Columbian) joined us. The idea of him joining us at the ball was too much for him but we were quickly running out of powder. I got the task of DJ, for which I was happy, and the party continued on for a couple of hours more. Several other people stopped in to grab a line or two but would leave soon after. Long after we had left planet earth Abigail decided to let me in on a secret about her sister- she liked rough sex. Abigail produced a luggage bag filled with sex toys and told me to fasten her sister to the bellman's cart. I wondered why that had been left there and had been trying to ride it like a skateboard about an hour before. She tossed me some handcuffs and leather straps. I saw Grace's thoughts on her face. At first, she thought it sounded like an enticing idea, but then looked around and realized she was in a room with her sister and a Columbian coke dealer. I think it was mostly the coke dealer that bothered her.

"Go ahead, ya' little slut! You know you want to!" Abigail coaxed Grace.

Grace quickly left her inhibitions, leapt up from our bed and pranced over to the luggage cart.

"You wanna'?" I asked her, giving her the chance to ask for an exit.

"Fuck yeah I do," she responded, which surprised me, but whatever... I was game.

I cuffed each wrist outstretched to either curved end of the bellman's cart as she stood on the platform.

"Take that dress off before you strap her ankles. It's not like she can say no," her sister teased.

I raised my eyebrows questioning her. She looked over at the coke dealer who was obviously making it a point to do anything except look over at us. He was more uncomfortable and more concerned about respect than Grace was.

Townsend

"Guy's, that is my cue to go. Enjoy and have a very good night," he said.

We all waved goodbye to him, including Grace, whose handcuffs rattled against the metal tubing when she waved.

"Crazy white people…" I heard him mutter on the way out.

I unzipped Grace's dress and slipped it down her legs as she remained crucified on the luggage cart. I could not find a place to fasten her ankles that the straps would reach, so I strapped her thighs to the center cross supports. I think she may have come when I locked the straps, leaving her legs spread. I looked down at her wet panties and was feeling an almost uncontrollable urge, except that it was controllable- I had constantly felt her sister and brother-in-law's presence over my shoulder. We both glanced over at them, they were not watching, Nick was on top of Abigail in the bed. I suddenly felt very sorry for the drug dealer and wondered how long Nick had been mounting his wife. We were all very far gone. I ran over to the light switch, turned off all but one lamp, and returned to Grace who was looking vulnerable. She was seething and salivating, so excited that she looked even

WORLDLY

drunker than she was. I kissed her heavily and felt her body, she bit my lip when I ran my hand between her legs. She let out a little groan, so I continued, and her thighs began to flex and shake.

"Put it in…" she whispered.

My desire far outweighed the taboo of the situation and I did as she asked. I unzipped my dress pants, moved her wet panties to one side and entered her. Grace came almost immediately, shaking so hard that the bellman's cart made a lot of clanking and we nearly tipped it over. I looked over my shoulder and made eye contact with her sister, who was watching over Nick's shoulder.

Grace and I were watched a few times mid-coitus; this was definitely a new thing to me. During a Saint Patrick's three-day binge, we stayed at Andrew and Michael's house. Grace and I came over to help remove Michael who had gotten in the habit of being extremely physically abusive to Andrew. Once that was handled, Andrew was really in the mood to get fucked up and we joined him. They had a nice big house but for some reason (that I do not recall) the first night we had passed out on the leather sofa in the living room.

Townsend

Something about being naked on a leather couch turned us on and we started going at it in the morning. Andrew, that horny bastard, kept making excuses to run into the room while we were having sex. We thought we were safe in privacy as it was early, but no. Seven A.M. and mid-coitus, naked Andrew needed to find the remote control. It was pretty funny, but he killed the mood for us. Andrew, Grace and I spent that weekend knee-deep in cocaine and wading through a pool of booze.

Saint Patrick's Day had given us a three-day weekend and that was the last fun I would know for a while… it was about to be a very bad week for me. I was at work performing my duties as a construction foreman and was out in the Bronco running to Home Depot to buy supplies for the jobsite. It had barely begun to rain, and the roads were slick. I took my time as I slowed for a stop in the left northbound lane for a light that had been red for some time. It changed to green.

Even with my windows up I heard tires sliding sideways on wet pavement. A woman in a Chevy Silverado traveling west hit the gas to try to beat her light that had just turned red. Instead of trying to blow straight through the intersection she still tried to make her left turn to go south but was going too fast. Her truck slipped on the wet roads and spun out of control. She crossed over my median and hit me head-to-head, totaling the Bronco.

I was OK, but the Bronco was not. I was now nearly alone in Texas and in danger of not having a vehicle. Her insurance paid for a rental and since I was in construction, it paid for a truck (things I knew to ask for since I had been a claims adjuster). So, I was back to work, briefly. A few days later I had a dentist appointment with my girlfriend. I loved my girlfriend, but I hated the dentist. It had been eight years since I had seen one. I had nice teeth, Grace said that was one of the things that attracted her to me.

Like everything else, I maintained my damn teeth myself, until I met Grace. Now I was obligated to be a regular in that chair as apparently, I was not doing a good enough job. I did have a few cavities but the big issue for her was my choice not to go back and get a crown and opted instead to wear the temporary for eight years (hey, they opened the door, and I ran out). Grace hated that I had gone eight years with just a flimsy temporary. She was itching to fix the thing which meant she had to give me a root canal on the gross old stump,

Townsend

take new impressions and make new temporary and permanent crown.

The day of the root canal I left work early and also took off the next day as Grace was not going to let me take any pain killers. She knew about my past, and also, as a doctor, she fucking hated opioids. She rightly thought those things were little doses of Satan's poo. The morning after the root canal I woke up on my right side with Grace in my arms. I lifted my head from the pillow but suddenly noticed there was a complete absence of sound. With Grace still asleep I proceeded to have a mini freak-out. I jammed my finger in my ear and smacked the right side of my head repeatedly. Nothing. I was completely deaf in my right ear. My mini freak-out turned into a full-on panic, and I woke up Grace as gently as I could.

"Babe... babe. Babe!"

"Whaaaaaaat?" Grace groaned as she squinted her eyes.

"I'm fuckin' deaf!" I whisper-yelled.

"What?" she asked, now mildly concerned.

WORLDLY

"I can't hear in my right ear!"

"Oh, your tooth just hurts. You're not deaf. You're over-reacting. Don't be a baby," she said and rolled over. "If this is a plot to get pain killers out of me it's not going to work."

"I'm pretty sure I'm deaf, babe!" I said, now questioning myself.

For all I knew she could have been right, I was no doctor. So, I set off to prove her right. I ran out of the room to find my cellphone. I'd left it charging on the kitchen counter the night before. I raised the volume all the way and found a *Rammstein* song, *Te Quero Puta*. I played it on speakerphone to get it as loud as possible. I heard Grace kick the bed, I don't believe there is a female alive that likes hearing *Rammstein* in the morning (and if there is, I would like to propose).

I held the phone to my left ear…sweet glorious music about putas.

I held it to my right ear… no sweet glorious music about putas.

I repeated my lab test and got the same result.

Townsend

"Babe… babe. Babe!" I said gently trying to wake Grace.

"Whaaaaaaat!" Grace groaned again, this time into a pillow and rolled over.

"*I'm fuckin' deaf*!" I screamed like I was on fire.

"No! *YOU ARE NOT!*" she screamed. "I'm a dentist! I am responsible for people's paychecks! I need my sleep and I have to work today! If you aren't going to let me sleep then leave my house!"

She played that card. My worst fear was homelessness and she threw it at me while she was half-asleep in her bed.

"What do I do to get you to help me? Call your emergency line and talk to your secretary?" I screamed, now extremely frustrated that she would not believe me.

That line did not sit well with Dr. Grace. She leapt from her bed and stormed out into the kitchen where I was slapping my head again.

"See I can't he…"

"Get out!" she screamed.

This was not what I expected.

"What? Hey I'm just... I can't hear. Can you tell me if this is normal at least? Wouldn't you be worried if you didn't know why you couldn't hear?" I plead.

"GET OUT!" she continued screaming.

"Babe... just tell me it's normal... you know what. It's fine. I have two ears."

Grace began picking up empty beer bottles from the kitchen countertop and hurling them at my head. I ducked, and they smashed against the front door of her apartment.

"GET OUT, GET OUT, GET OUT!" she screamed hysterically.

I ran in to the bedroom, threw on my work clothes and even though I had the day off, went the only other place in Texas I had to go, work.

Townsend

Now, not only did my tooth hurt but the whole side of my head hurt. I was just glad I ducked the bottles or else my whole head may have hurt. I parked outside of the jobsite and texted Grace, I told her I was sorry for yelling, that I was just scared. I went in to work and did not hear anything from her. I told the guys at work what happened, and they thought it was hilarious, but they did not have to live it. My boss said I could crash at his house if Grace really was done with me. The pounding of hammers and power tools was killing me, so I resolved to sit in the rental truck until I either felt better or Grace called.

Around lunchtime I got a call from a guy who said he was friends with Grace, an endodontist. He called me in and somehow, he already knew the whole story. He was a young man but a couple years older than we were.

"She can be something, huh?" Dr. Khatri said, laughing when he came into the operatory.

Dr. Khatri took X-rays and found I was getting an infection, and the root canal had not been done properly. The infection swelled tissue and put pressure on a nerve that caused me to lose hearing in my ear. He re-did the root canal, gave me anti-biotics, and because he also thought my plight was hilarious, wrote me a prescription for a huge bottle of pain killers. Grace had specifically demanded when they spoke that he not do that, but he A.) didn't give a shit... and B.) knew I was hurting since the infection was bad enough for me to temporarily lose my hearing.

"Here, don't let her push you around," he said laughing at my expense.

Dr. Khatri seemed to know something I did not. They had gone to dental school together and they chatted on the regular, sending patients back and forth. I wish he would have just told me what he was laughing about. I went to the pharmacy and filled the prescriptions when I finally got a text from Grace:

Sunshine On A Cloudy Day

Come home right after

the endo.

Townsend

I will tell you something, I took a pain killer before I got back there, I just had two back-to-back root canals. When I got home she immediately jumped down my throat about the pain killers. I even asked her (as my dentist) if I could please take them because my head was falling off, but she almost had another conniption, so I ran into the bathroom with them.

"Hey! You have a problem with them? Fine! I'll flush the fuckin' problem down the toilet!" I yelled.

I ripped open the bottle of pain killers and flushed them down the toilet (after I pocketed about ten of them out of spite). She really liked that I got mad and flushed them down the toilet. She was fine after that; the storm had passed, and the cloudy day was over. I was glad for it.

The rental truck was only good for a week after they offered me a settlement. I did not except the first settlement amount and provided a giant folder of every receipt uber-organized Joey had saved on the upgrades and work done on the Bronco. This doubled the settlement check and I now had a down payment for a new truck.

WORLDLY

Grace went with me to look for a truck. We went to Ford, but my credit sucked. I had been sleeping on couches and partying for years, "seeing the world". I hadn't worried about building credit, I did not even know how it worked. We went to Chevy and I got turned down again. Finally, we went to Dodge.

"Fuck it, we'll give you a truck," said Dodge. "We'll give you a used truck that's still new enough to cost almost thirty-thousand dollars and then we are going to try to murder you with interest."

The guy at Dodge was a gangster. Grace was getting tired of going truck shopping with me and was just happy someone finally said they would finance me. We found a truck that both of us liked, a charcoal 2012 Ram 1500 extended cab. It had a flip-down TV in the cab, Flowmaster exhaust, and chrome rims. By far the nicest vehicle I had ever even hoped to own.

When discussing the loan arrangements, the monthly payment they offered just about knocked me out of my seat. Of course, they had our impulses for ransom and we wanted that truck, so the guy asked about Grace's credit which she offered up like we were married. I did not want Grace on my

Townsend

vehicle's title, it was way too early in the relationship and we had just experienced fights that went to levels I did not know possible. Regardless, the payment was over a hundred dollars a month cheaper with her dentist-credit and she was almost talking me into it. So, we bought the truck. Less than a year into a relationship and she was on my truck's title and I was responsible for the payment. Even with her co-signature the payment was almost five hundred dollars a month. I would come to regret not buying something outright from the classifieds. If our relationship soured, Grace had a big card to play.

Grace and I continued to play house and we attempted to build a life together. Ever since the root canal incident I had a hard time trusting her, as for the first six months I never knew she had the potential to fly off the handle like that. As time went on I learned that a little monster lived inside of her, a monster she did her best to try and conceal from people in public and at work. She lacked self-control and was not always successful. Anyone who was close to her, including her own family, knew it existed. A problem was quickly growing and coming to a head, I loved Grace. When she was happy and smiling she had the power to make me love life, when she was not, I despised every breath I took. I really knew no one else in Texas so, wherever the Grace rollercoaster was on the track, I was strapped in for the ride.

Now that our lives revolved around each other, Grace decided she no longer had a need for going out drinking. Our social life quickly diminished and was replaced with a health-obsessed lifestyle. We did not eat much red meat, unless we went out to eat, in which case I might splurge on a steak. Grace instead looked for meat "replacements". This led to pretty much every normal ingredient being replaced by some health food that tasted like stale shit.

She once made spaghetti with spaghetti squash instead of actual noodles (apparently noodles are also poison). In reality most of the meals she made tasted great when it was her turn to cook, but I had to throw in the towel half way through that one. She also started regularly going to the gym which to me is one of the most menial tasks there is. I can understand going to the gym to work out if you have an office job, but I lifted weight every day building things. If you want to repeatedly lift a hundred pounds, then feel free to bring me some lumber from Home Depot. When I got home from work I was already physically exhausted and the last thing I wanted to do was go

Townsend

drain myself further. Grace hated this and her tactic to try and get me in the gym was that she might meet someone else at the gym and cheat on me, so I had better be there to prevent it. That tactic did not work. The way I see it is if someone had the ability to cheat on me then I would rather they just did, so I know what they are capable of and move on. The changes Grace wanted in themselves are positive things, but the problem was in how it was implemented... which was almost religious obsession.

The trust between us was suffering. I would repeatedly catch Grace digging through my phone. Thinking I may cheat was ridiculous, I knew no one in Texas. The only people I did spend time with was her family and her father was my best friend. Despite that fact, for some reason my loyalty was still a liability to her.

I eventually took a job that her brother-in-law, Nick, had offered. He was the president of a popular home improvement company and he got me a good job as an estimator. So, I spent my days driving all over north Texas to estimate. One day I had a long trip ahead of me to the next estimate and had to use the bathroom. Being a picky pooper, I stopped home to use the bathroom and got a text message from Grace while sat on the porcelain throne.

Sunshine On A Cloudy Day

Where are you?

Jason

Working. Have to run to Decatur.

Sunshine On A Cloudy Day

No, you're not. Why are you

lying to me?

Jason

What??

Sunshine On A Cloudy Day

You are full of shit. Why are

you at the house instead of at

Townsend

work?

Jason

I had to poo before driving for

an hour...

Sunshine On A Cloudy Day

Right.

Jason

How do you know where

I am right now?

I later discovered that Grace had downloaded an app on to my phone that would allow her to track me. So, while she was at work, instead of working on patients, she sat on her computer and tracked my fucking whereabouts. Even though this infuriated me, I tried to internalize it and failed. I kept thinking about the beer bottles thrown at my half-deaf head. I could not stop thinking about the breach of privacy and sneaky spy tactics. What bothered me even more was that she felt like she had to do to it in the first place... and I could not understand what I had done to earn that. This was starting to feel like my parents' house, being searched daily for contraband.

When I got home, Grace was already in defense-mode, gloves laced up and ready to fight. It did not take long to spiral out of control and the fight got physical. After she clawed me and left long scratches down my face and neck I decided to go outside to let things calm down. When I tried to come back inside and make up, the door was dead bolted, the kind that does not have a key and can only be locked from the inside. I knocked on the door for half an hour before giving up and ended up spending the night in my truck.

The next day I apologized, did not receive one in return, and went back to normal life with Grace. Of all the red flags this is one that sticks with me, an intelligent and agreeable person should be able to apologize to another human being and not feel they are hurting themselves. On the contrary, someone who has the ability to reflect on their own actions and adjust is an evolving human being. Unfortunately, most

Townsend

of my apologies to Grace also were usually not genuine, they were done through my teeth to keep the peace and live to see another day. I guess I am not a very alert and evolving human either.

I did respect Grace's will to improve. Her effort however was directed at the surface and the major problems were left overlooked. Grace's monster of stress and anger never received any attention to fix, instead any effort put into it was spent trying to pretend it did not exist- like a giant carnivorous elephant in the room. I suggested therapy once as nicely as I could, giving a preamble that what I was about to say came from a place of love and willingness to grow as a couple. It ended up turned back at me, with *me* signing up for therapy at a church. Grace tried to make us look as if we were actively improving, by shopping at expensive health food stores, living in an overly expensive high-rise apartment, going to a public gym, and going on vacations to pump out seemingly happy and healthy pictures for all social media to see, meanwhile the foundation of the relationship was infested with termites.

My least favorite and menial surface attempt to fix our problems was suddenly joining a church. Grace was well aware of how I was brought up and my growing views on atheism but insisted we join a typical Texas stadium church. Texas has a brand of religion that rarely exists outside of the south due to its ridiculous nature, and I joined one to keep Grace happy. These churches embody everything I find horribly hypocritical about modern religion. The church we picked had a rock band that played Christian "hard rock", the dress was casual, the stage had huge flat screen televisions, an HD projector, expensive lighting, an insane sound system with a god-sized subwoofer, and seating for thousands. Oh, how the thousands flocked to this display.

The place dripped with an obvious desperate and gaudy attempt to modernize archaic religion and touted Jesus camps for the kids, celibacy camps for the teens and more tech than some entire countries have.

At the start of every service, the lights were dimmed and the amplifiers cranked as the rock band sang power ballads dedicated to the crucified Lord. The lyrics were displayed across the enormous theater screen as the teary-eyed audience sang along in between fits of emotional break downs. I noticed that the way the place was set up was actually *designed* to be a cry factory and incite emotions, since this appears to be the influence of the Holy Spirit. Churches like this are built to overwhelm the senses with loud emotional music, light shows, and empty-headed touchy-feely congregation members. The children were always filed away in their religious daycare as the music was too loud for young ears, which also allowed the parents not to be distracted from the message being drilled in by way of sensory overload. Parents are less likely to ball their eyes out with their children at their side.

The pastor was like a rock star, a young guy who dressed like a department store model. He was carefully chosen as someone the entire congregation either wanted or wanted to be. The tactic was so successful that even while my skeptical self was in a church service I would find myself getting into it, until the car ride home when I realized the shallowness of the attempted force-feeding. You could not very well criticize what you were being told until you were on your way home and able to think for yourself again (surely the work of the Devil).

Grace tried to sell this to me as something I should be interested in, because in fact, "they do not consider themselves a religion". She wanted me to just have faith- a word worshipped, that means to believe something without evidence. This is something that if done in pretty much any other area would be considered ignorance. This money-making, people-organizing system was also a non-denominational army of armed Texans for Jesus. It seems that as time goes on even religion is noticing that the word "religion" is vernacular best hidden in a drawer with the other labels. The fact remains that no matter how they modernized this decidedly archaic system, at its core it remained the same exact thing I was raised in and ripped apart my family. It was a tithing machine built to chain people by their heartstrings to guilt to make a profitable place for people to feel they have all of the answers to the universe... and the answers are coincidentally beneficial to man.

Still, I kept my feelings on the matter internalized and tried, for Grace and the sake of peace, to be an agreeable lemming. I even tried to squeeze a tear or two out for her and the pastor.

At this point I was internalizing so many things for the sake of seeing another peaceful day that I felt myself bursting at the seams and was worried I could not hold it together, but it made it easier to cry in public. Grace had done some positive things for me, I was no longer getting fucked up regularly to

Townsend

forget about my past. Instead the damage was being done in real time and I had no choice but to stare it right in the eyes with no way to dull the realization that I was a fish out of water. I was terrified to fail, if I was not meant to be with Grace in Dallas then I did not know where I was meant to be anymore, I was fresh out of new places to run.

Grace was getting comfortable with flying off the handle and was doing it regularly. At one point, while having dinner at her parent's house it got so bad that I decided right then and there to leave and go back to California. I ran to the truck but Grace ran out, wedged herself in between the truck and the driver's door, took my keys in her hand and repeatedly punched me in the face.

Her mother ran out and just stood there looking ashamed of her daughter but did not try to step in. I wished that for probably the first time in Grace's life, her mother would take her over her knee and spank her. I could not hit her back. Instead I took about fifteen to twenty shots to the face before I grabbed her by the wrists and held them until she gave up, pulling my keys from her hand. I could have left right then and gone back to rebuilding a life suited for me, instead I pulled over only a few miles down the road and decided I was not yet ready to fail at another relationship. I was not even sure where to flee to, New York or California? I had friends in both states. San Diego for the weather? Either way I would be starting over now in my thirties and would be a burden to whatever friend offered help.

The next day Grace made me apologize for the bruises around her wrists where I restrained her from hitting me (and didn't get one back).

By this time, I was miserable. I looked forward to sleep as an escape from reality. Grace had me believe I was sick and abusive, but really it was the other way around. I felt imprisoned in the state of Texas. Monotony has a way of making you feel trapped. The routine of going to work and going home can be scary to leave, because you will always reason "at least I have a job and roof over my head". I came to realize I had willingly walked into a situation very similar to the one I fought to leave before adulthood. Someone was trying to force me into a mold I did not belong in. I was constantly under attack by the same person who said they loved me, making me believe I was wrong in everything I did and thought. I dreaded going home from work. It got so bad that I felt like a weight was off me every minute I was away

Townsend

from Grace, and I felt in danger every time she was in my presence.

Few people are ever excited and thankful to go to the dentist, which is not her fault. Usually they act like scared babies, as if them jumping in to the dentist chair is doing more of a favor to the dentist. She constantly dealt with pain and misery every day, but she brought that home. The only enjoyment we mutually received from her practice was on the day we went in after hours, got lit up on nitrous, had sex in her office and left for a concert. That was about the only thing we did well.

Grace's mother told me that she was under too much stress from buying her own practice right out of college, and this is why she was so moody. She learned to be a dentist, but they did not teach business management. The stress of being an employer was getting to her and I could clearly see that, she would not let me forget it. Her stress was my stress. Eventually Grace's parents convinced her to sell her practice to an older doctor and stay on as a dentist. She sold the practice, a long and even more stressful process as she had problems with him too, but there was little change. My attempt at sobriety was wearing thin. I would drink when we went out to do something, but during normal days I tried to act like a normal person and stay sober.

Grace always got home from work before I did, this made me always dread the end of the work day. I hoped for traffic. It got so bad that I began routinely stopping after work to get the most alcoholic tall can I could find, and drink two on the commute home. Once home I would sit in my parking space and chew whole pack of gum to try and hide the smell. Half the time she would catch the smell on my breath and it would still lead to a fight. I would do it anyway because the fighting was more tolerable when I was drunk, and I could fall asleep easier.

The fighting became brutal, and the part that really disturbed me was that when she fought, she would smile. She seemed a natural fighter. This ended up with her telling me to leave her house, so I gladly packed up. Her parents invited me to stay at their house.

I really enjoyed staying at her parents'. I was too old to be doing such a thing, but they were enjoyable, positive people. I had no idea how Grace could be their product. Her dad did drink almost every day, but he was never sloppy, and

Townsend

he had a good marriage with his wife. He had a few beers every day starting at dinner, usually with his wife. Grace said he was an alcoholic and was worried I would end up like him. He was a simple and happy guy who worked with his hands and liked to shoot guns. Guns were something I knew little about having lived in New York and California. I hoped to end up like him. I just wanted to be happy and live in peace like he did with his wife. They got along and did not fight. They liked most everyone, if there was a political figure they did not care for they would not yell and scream at the TV, they would just make jokes and laugh it off. They were not rich, Grace had to reluctantly help her parents a few times with money, but they always had a smile and they always helped us in any way they could. In my opinion they were rich in a way I longed for, but Grace did not see it that way.

Whenever things were bad between Grace and I they had positive advice that did not hurt either party. They always made me feel as if things would get better and I would try to hold on. I lived with them for well over a month after Grace kicked me out and I was becoming happier. I felt more at home with them and I could be myself. They liked new ideas, they did not make me go to church and they were humble. I

WORLDLY

had dinner with them every night, we would laugh and watch a documentary. Grace would come over once a week for dinner and during that time I was banished to hide in my room until she left. After weeks of pep talks I started to miss the things I loved about Grace and forget the massive problems. I missed her beautiful face and missed lying in bed with her. I missed the occasions when she was happy and fun. She had an infectious laugh that I wished I heard more often. She loved when I did my Hank Hill impression, and we wrote an entire duet in the voices of Hank and Peggy, but that joke quickly wore off. I had milked it dry.

After weeks of analyzing the problems we had, her mom thought Grace was concerned I would leave her. That is an understandable concern, I had moved a lot in the past, and tried to leave her once already. So, we decided I should ask her to marry me, thus giving her security.

Grace and I made up and I moved back in with her. She had a dental conference coming up in San Francisco and I was going with her. I planned to ask her to marry me during that trip, but it was weeks away.

Townsend

Her mother gave me an engagement ring that an ex-boyfriend had given her before that relationship fell through. I could not afford a better one any quicker. I went to Polaroid and had thick cards made up of all of our best photos and printed labels of when and where they were. I put them together in chronological order, the last photo being of a sunset we watched together titled "Will You Marry Me?". I punched two holes and used bow string to tie the ring to the picture. I planned to show her the permanent pictures I had made up of our best memories while at a lobster dinner and show her the last card from bended knee.

Grace's mom was right; she was getting increasingly upset that I had not asked her to marry me. We had been together less than two years and I wanted to take my time. By the time we got to our hotel in San Francisco she was irate.

"You are never going to ask me to marry you! You are just using me for my money!" she screamed at me before I had even unpacked. "Fuck, I am so stupid! You were only supposed to be a one-night stand! I should have just let it be!"

"What?" I dropped what I was doing in shock.

"Yeah. Andrew and Lisa set me up with you because you were going through a divorce and we both needed a rebound. My stupid ex cheated on me, your stupid Puerto Rican ex cheated on you. We were supposed to have sex and that was it. You were supposed to go back to San Diego and I would move on, but no. We had to fall in fucking love. I am so stupid."

"I was supposed to be a one-night-stand?" I asked.

For some reason this hurt. It kind of made sense but at the time it just hurt, and that is exactly why she said it. She always went right for the jugular.

She threw a few more threats at me including I should once again move out when we got home if I was not serious about our future. This escalated to the point that I lost my temper, showed her the Polaroid cards I had in my bag, and threw the ring at her. One thing you did not want to do is make Grace feel stupid or that you had won a fight, because she would make life even worse if she felt trapped in the wrong. I climbed back up the mountain to once again make peace with Grace. While rain beat down outside, dinner that night had a cringe-worthy feeling in the air, the surprise ruined. I proposed to her while recovering from a fight and she accepted.

Grace and I joined a month-long marriage boot camp at the stadium church. This boot camp boasted to increase the chances of marriage survival so significantly that the state of Texas would waive the marriage fee if the class was passed. The class dug up every dark corner of a relationship including finances and gave advice on how to handle relationship-breaking problems. It also made an open attempt to break relationships right there in the class, so only the strong survived (an evolutionary tactic). Hundreds of couples started the class and less than half stuck it out and survived until the end, receiving the church's blessing. Don't ask me how, but we were one of them.

The ups and downs of planning a wedding were weighing on us so we took a cruise from Miami to Cozumel, Mexico and back. I drank more than I probably should have but by this time I was becoming increasingly concerned about it. Grace had me join a type of alcoholics anonymous at the stadium church but felt its generic advice was so far from me that I could not even fake that it resonated. What did stick with me again, were the people there who had stories of drinking while in bad relationships, the real stories from real people. It haunted me, and it was becoming ever clearer that I had to look in the mirror and face a real problem.

Late one night during our trip the boat alarm sounded, I jumped out of bed and ran to the top deck to see we had come across a Cuban trying to flee and floating on an inner tube in the middle of the ocean. As I looked down at him, floating in the huge open sea while our ship tried to rescue him, I never felt I identified with someone more. By the time we left the cruise ship the excitement of the vacation was over and we fought again.

Grace and I continued to fight after we got home. Planning a wedding just added more fuel to the fire. We saw several different venues until we just stopped looking. Eventually I was so miserable that I started to consider suicide again as an out, so I left Grace.

By this time Nick and I were running our own remodeling company and he invited me to stay with him. I stuck it out for about a month. I met Grace at a bar one night to talk but I knew it was over. I had exhausted every opportunity for this to work and it simply was not going to.

Townsend

I'd lost Tim and Lisa, they had long been married and I didn't even go to their wedding.

I learned the hard way that I had made a bad investment and gave every opportunity for three years to find a way to hold on and find happiness together. Nothing ever got better, it only got worse and more abusive, and the longer I stayed the more she tried to destroy my self-esteem. No matter how she tried, I would not be told I was worthless. I had a fight in me that only can be learned through extreme survival.

I wanted to hold on to the first night at The Grapevine forever, but it was long gone. I wanted to break a cycle of running, assuming that is why I had not been successful in a relationship. I could do anything, but I could not do this anymore.

Nick saw my depression spiral, I was now becoming a hermit holed up in his windowless movie theater and drinking myself to sleep every night, waking only to go to work and repeat. I was so scared and there was no other way for me to fall asleep but to pass out. Nick and Abigail had children, and this was nothing for them to see, a mangy dude with wine-stained teeth.

WORLDLY

I pulled myself up by my bootstraps, after all I had been homeless before, and packed my truck. I worried a bit as I would have to get right to work to pay my expensive truck bill every month. I called Joey in San Diego who offered his couch and assured I would be able to find work. The night before I was about to leave I had Nicks house to myself and was finally feeling the light of positivity had come back in to my world; it was called hope. As bad as things can be you can always hope for better and no one can take that from you. I excitedly called my friends in San Diego and made plans to see them soon. Then a tow truck pulled up in the ally and hooked up to my packed truck. I ran outside with my gun and jumped in the driver's seat before it could be removed. The tow truck driver said he had papers to repossess the truck for non-payment. This had to be wrong, the last two months I gave Grace the cash so she could make the payments. Of course, I did not get a receipt from my fiancé.

I held the driver at gunpoint and called the police to let them know what was happening. They showed up, checked his paperwork and verified that it looked legitimate. The tow truck driver felt sorry for me and let me unpack my truck and put my belongings back into Nick's garage. One of the police officers also felt bad for me and decided to call Grace to get the other side of the story.

"Damn, man. She's cold," is the response I received from him as he shrugged his shoulders.

Whatever Grace did to take my truck and make it harder for me to leave, I am glad she did. Looking back now, she really did me a favor. Joey had some spare miles on his airline credit card and bought me a flight the next day.

I told Nick about the flight only hours before it left and I reluctantly accepted a ride to the airport. I was getting paranoid and did not know who I could trust. I apologized to Nick later and he understood, the man was a good friend to me. He gave me a place to stay when I was down and out, and he continued to store my things for six months after I left until I could come get them. Grace picked through it, but it was a small price to pay. Most of all he did not sugar coat that I was in over my head with his sister-in-law, and gave me good advice. Nick dropped me off at the airport where I left with two bags to start over again. He made me feel I could do better, and he was right.

WORLDLY

The point of this part of the story is not the mistakes Grace made or that she is a bad person. Grace and I were just not right for each other and were very different people in the wrong places of our lives. In fact, we may have never shown interest in each other in the first place if we met at better places in our lives, or (less possibly) it may have worked. It is about the mistakes I made, there is a bigger picture here.

I left Texas for California on a Monday.

Townsend

CHAPTER SIXTEEN

<u>The Big Bang</u>

Once back in San Diego, Joey helped me get on my feet. He gave me a couch to sleep on and within two weeks I was working. My first job was remodeling a high-rise penthouse over-looking Shelter Island. Every day on lunch break I would eat out on the balcony and be thankful I was not in Texas. I was thankful I got out of there instead of taking the easy way out. The bright sun, sea gulls, palm trees and boats from a birds-eye view made me feel happy to be alive. It was like finally getting casts removed from both legs.

My rock bottom did not come to me lying in a hospital bed, or peering out of the bars of a jail cell. It came to me in Texas. My rock bottom was somehow ending up back in my childhood home again, failing miserably at pretending I belonged and running away again to start over. I was now thirty-one years old, and I still did not have "the right girl" and it was time to think about what my life was to become. How could I answer an ad on a dating site and bring someone back to my friend's couch? Why would I even want to? How could I entertain the idea of being with another person if I had nothing to offer but problems that needed fixed?

A glaring problem had existed my entire adult life and a clue was right in front of me the whole time. Annabelle moved in almost as soon as I got my first apartment. I lived on couches in California. I lived with Grace almost immediately in Texas. I jumped from one girlfriend to the next since I ran away from home as a teenager. I was terrified to be alone with myself. I had run three-thousand miles only to find out my problems were stuck to my heel. I sped up the pace of the world by staying busy working and drinking. When you dumb down your brain it seems as if you are doing more. You are just ignoring a problem. It does not matter who you are, if you are drinking every day there is a problem. It may be something deeply emotional you are trying to dull. At the very least the habitual drinking is a problem. I had not slept in my car finishing high school just to fall apart later in life. I had survived a hell of a lot so far.

Townsend

When asking some tough questions, I saw that I was making myself a victim of circumstance. Like most victims of circumstance, I perpetuated my own problems, and I was really the one that needed to be held responsible, not Grace, not Annabelle, not even my parents. As a grown man, an imperfect rearing did not matter anymore. I had to fix myself and do it for *myself*. When faced with the question of what my future may be, I stopped drinking overnight. Ten years of heavy drinking stopped overnight because of one word: survival, and it was almost easy.

Circumstances had been trying to take me out for twenty years, I did not need to help them. I looked at myself through the lens of everyone who knew me. I wondered what my parents would think, who had no interest in even calling me. I wanted to drink so I would fit in with a bar full of peers and make more friends. I started smoking cigarettes so that I seemed less like a Jehovah's Witness and more "worldly". One day I said *fuck it,* fuck what everyone else thinks of me, I need to be able to like myself.

A few years ago, I stopped looking for a partner to make me feel whole. All I have ever wanted is a woman I loved to scratch my back when I feel the world is crushing in on me. I had to learn over time that I do not need one. Just because I can get one does not mean that I should. My mother is gone, no one can replace her, and no one ever will. Today's life is filled with apps and websites designed to help us meet the perfect partner, just check a box, but at the same time more and more young people are choosing to be single. I do not specifically intend on trying to be a Tyler Durden from *Fight Club* by saying 'fuck it' to a relationship forever, I would like to meet my Marla. What I am saying is that I do not care if I don't.

The path I set out in made me race through a lifetime of experiences in a decade and it is high time for a breather. If you try to do too much at once you miss the point. I stopped worrying about trying to share my problems with someone and instead have taken years off to fix the problems. I took up every hobby I ever wanted to do but couldn't because I had no time. I learned guitar, I rebuilt two boats and I wrote a book. I became a doer instead of a plan-to-doer. That was an excellent choice. I stopped sprinting through life, the dust has settled, and now I can look back and correct my form.

San Diego is an expensive place, even without a bar tab. I had bought a thirty-foot boat floating in America's Cup in

Townsend

Shelter Island. At the time you could live all utilities included for five-hundred dollars a month. What I once paid to have a shiny new truck could pay for the roof over my head. I woke up every day, looked out the windshield of my boat and took in the sight of sailboats passing the north tip of Coronado Island. I felt like the luckiest guy on earth, and I was happily alone. The boat was a wonderful place to write. When you slow life down it is easier to appreciate the finer things that you normally whizz right past. The phrase- "stop and smell the roses"- cannot be overstated. I think this is the reason most wealthy people complain of not being happy, they are moving too fast and are distracted.

In this modern world of communication, it is hard to hear yourself think, and if you cannot think, then how do you expect to know yourself? I took up photography and tried to capture little individual moments. I would slow life down to a still frame. Previously if I found myself unable to sleep in the middle of the night I would drink until I passed out. Now I would buzz around in a solar-powered dinghy I built and go take pictures on the still water.

I found an old row boat, fixed it up, added a trolling motor, battery, solar panel and voila, self-sufficient boat that needs no gas for roughly $300. I lived in peace. At night there is a time where San Diego Bay is still and the water looks like glass. The moon and skyline reflect off the water's surface, and to me that is the most beautiful sight there is in the whole city. I was very aware while I was living on a boat that I was having 'a time' of my life. There is no such thing as '*the* time of your life'; it's only that way if you give up. Your life should be a series of times of your life. I came from a very low place in Dallas, and within months rapidly shot up to living the happiest life I'd ever had by managing expectations.

I slowed down at work too. If I stopped rushing to get done and paid so I could go blow the money at a bar, then I could enjoy what I was doing. Any job is a craft not everyone can do well. Charge by the job, not the hour, and take your time. You do your job better than most people, and that is why they pay *you* to do it. Working with my hands felt good to my soul. When your life has been systematically dismantled from the start, it gives you a sense of worth to be able to build something new with your hands. There is something carnally pleasing about the ability to craft something tangible. I found a particular joy in building or fixing up another person's home, where they will enjoy it for years to come. I also simply

Townsend

appreciate the tools themselves, along with the projects they helped to build.

Living on a boat in San Diego was not only awesome, but it saved me a lot of money. I was able to invest the money I earned in tools for my craft. Once that was adequate, I was able to rent my own small house, sell the big thirty-foot boat, and pass the memory machine to the next person going through a divorce. I never had or cared to have much money. I think if I had lived my whole life without saving a penny, on my deathbed I would look back and feel I did something unknowingly wise. I was taught in my religion that to become rich is to basically hoard money, and that has been hard to shake. I do not spend as much time as I probably should be worrying about money. The end of my life is not going to be spent shoveling money into the medical industry to lengthen my weakening life, but I will have saved some money to pass on to my children. When the time comes, the end of my life will cost less than a dollar, to me that is a very freeing thought that helps me enjoy the present.

So, what is the point of all this? Why did you read this book? Bear with me, I am almost done and hopefully you will pick it out for yourself. I spent a lot of years angry at my parents for not giving me the tools to coexist with real people in the real world. It is true that sheltering your child will only hinder their chances of survival when they leave home. I am living proof, but I am also living proof that you can overcome shitty parenting. Your chance in finding happiness depends on yourself. It depends how much you expect from life and how much you are willing to work to get it. If you were dealt a short straw, you may have to work a little harder to succeed; in turn your successes (no matter how small) will be sweeter. You will surely enjoy success more when you find it because you earned it yourself when you were actively rooted against. I never felt content with the idea of spending this whole life looking towards the next one like my parents did.

I chose to work for happiness, now, in this life. It was not always that way, as I spent a lot of time looking backward. When you spend all your time looking backward you cannot see what is coming at you, and you are liable to trip. I tripped and fell for ten years.

I have battled depression almost my entire life. It is a difficult thing to reject the happy promise of life ever after and accept that we are terminal- this is why my religion was created in the first place. Time has whittled me down and pieces of me lie scattered in various places across the planet. Panic and stress have riddled and poked holes in any steady happiness I may have ever retained with another human being. They say ignorance is bliss and there is significant truth in that saying, but it also stifles progress. In the year 200 A.D. Hua Tuo discovered the first sedative effective enough to allow the evolution of surgery, but this went against Confucius's teachings and Hua Tuo burned his medical journals, setting advancement back eight-hundred years. My troubles began the day I started to question the modern religious convention I was raised in, but I did not want to end up like Hua Tuo. I found beautiful breakthroughs in my own self that my parents would have me stifle for the sake of falling in line to tradition. The problem with seeing too much of the world is not knowing how to make sense of it all. There are more questions than there are answers in life. My parents found stability in their lives by accepting cozy prefab answers and by choosing to spend their entire life looking for ways to prove another man's ideas correct, instead of challenging their world's authenticity. To me that is just a sedative for enduring life, and life should be treated with more respect.

WORLDLY

Their religion is a platform of safety upon which they feel above everyone that disagrees. They are terrified of anything that may threaten to knock them off that platform of safe, beautiful ignorance. The problem with curiosity is that it leads to more questions, and questions do not keep you warm at night. I have sought questions my whole life. My curiosity destroyed my family life and led me into dangers that I have narrowly survived, but it is who I am and I would never trade it. My natural attraction to the questionable has made life confusing and I have had a hard time finding direction. After all, what profession exists for a person with a bunch of questions? A writer for one. After years of asking hard questions and finding hard answers a picture begins to form, a picture many people are beginning to see as humanity continues to evolve. It is those that continue to question and are consequently able to change who evolve the human race, not those who are content standing still.

I tortured myself with drugs and alcohol trying to run from a past I deemed unfair. However, my parents did care enough to do what they *thought* was right for me. They were not lying to me because they actually believed what they were preaching and teaching. They just did not have the fortitude to dig outside of what *they* were taught as children and for whatever reason they did not need to. I truly hope they have lived happy lives.

All in all, I moved thirty-eight times within five states. I moved a lot of times and met a lot of different people and have heard their life perspectives. I try to use all the information I have learned as a data-base, trying to understand what we are doing here. At the very least we are doing what every other living organism does, populating and living our lives. Being on top of the food chain we are afforded the pleasure of being aware of our lives, this can also be a curse. I do not want to waste my life being angry about the past or looking to a promise of a redo. I want to learn as much I can about people and I want to leave this planet better (and more informed) than it was when I found it. That is enough for me.

How can I put faith in something that has been repeatedly proven wrong? In my family house evolution was truly a dirty word, yet with a little education its existence is infallible. The wide availability of educational material has forced religions like mine to change and adapt over time. You could say that "The Truth" itself has evolved.

There are fish with wings that can fly. The Capuchin is a monkey that prepares its food and effectively reuses refined tools to split palm seeds. Turbot is a missing-link fish that is in the process of evolving from a vertical to horizontal fish with eyes on one side but a mouth left sideways. In my simple opinion, the word "faith" is the antitheses of education, and this is based on what I have learned hands-on, by rationally trying to prove religion correct. I strongly believe in a human being's natural right to evolve- a right defined by life itself. The next logical move for religion is to evolve and learn to integrate evolution into its doctrine, that the Creator created life *to* evolve. We must remember the facts: time after time religion has been blatantly proved wrong as our collective intelligence has grown; it must not be let off the hook this time. Religions have ripped families and nations apart for too long. Religions are book critics that band together over a fine piece of literature. The authors of this book were ahead of their time, but not ahead of ours. They were intelligent and evolving beings that were able to analyze patterns in history, make predictions based on logic and explain them as divinity.

This still happens, Joseph Smith pulled a divine caper roughly a hundred years ago. L. Ron Hubbard did it in just 1952. How long are we going to fall for this? How long must we cling to this faulty lack of science in order to maintain the narcissistic view that we are important, special organisms and will live forever in blissful nirvana? Why do we feel we need answers so badly that we must fabricate them and gather followers to feel validated? The first thing mankind learned to do was to war. Religion is a type of army that recruits as many to its uniform as possible, not all armies drop bombs. I was once an army recruiter for the Jehovah's Witnesses, marching door to door trying to enlist The Worldly in my placebo army of ignorance. I offered a lifetime of servitude in exchange for a life-long opioid high, that one day there will be "no more death or mourning or crying or pain, for the former things have passed away". This was my first experience as a type of child drug dealer.

I do not believe in a God in Heaven due to my own personal research, journey and lack of scientific evidence but I also do not have all the answers. If convincing scientific evidence showed up tomorrow that a God created us to evolve and created the expanding universe in a rapid explosion billions of years ago I would change and adapt my views. If they prove that math is just a coincidental perspective that only explains a fraction of something that adds up to creation, then I would adapt, and admit it is possible. For now, however, I trust the educated physicists and cosmologists who draw from centuries of science, not religious leaders who draw from faith and 1,200 pages written only 2,700 years ago. The same pages that claim the entire food chain was once floating on a global flood in a wooden ark with an incestuous family that re-mothered all races of humanity. Come on, now.

To be curious is to embrace the fiber that makes us human. Religion tells us not to be curious but to accept outdated reasoning and become a follower of men. My family's religion instructs people to choose their religion over their own family (that does not agree spiritually) and I have a cosmic-sized problem with that.

Self-realization and curiosity is what has made the human race expand just as the galaxy does. As long as we continue to ask questions we continue to be an active participator of the galaxy. I believe there is a reason religion has been deeply involved in, and has tried to stifle scientific progress- to stay ahead of the 8-ball and mold it as it sees fit. However, I am not trying to organize a group of people against religion, this is only my hypothesis. I just want them educated (and held responsible for sex crimes that are systemically

Townsend

covered up). I simply want fellowship across a broader audience and to wake up a large group of lost individuals (who would consider me so).

There absolutely was a good reason the biblical content was written, and it is deeper than just the narcissistic and shallow hope to live forever in perfection. There are giant, tangible issues that we need to come together and work on now, such as, global warming, fossil fuel consumption, carbon dioxide and methane emissions, changes in vital ocean currents and sea life, poor and overextended food sources, water shortages, overpopulation, greed, racism, sexism, and prejudice to indigenous peoples who's "uncivilized" lives never caused these problems. It was the "civilized" whose industry is destroying our home for all at an unprecedented pace and religion has a big hand in it. We need to evolve in a way that allows future generations to work on these problems as well. There is no redo for planet Earth, and we caused this. The changes necessary to succeed come from within ourselves and our parenting of children who understand the real concerns. The content religion uses is actually the glue that holds us together *now*, moral fiber... love. So why is religion driving us apart?

WORLDLY

Today I watched a video on social media. This one was of a dog (captured on hidden camera) while the owner was away. The dog was forbidden to be on the owner's bed. Can you guess what the dog did while the owner was away? The dog found bliss in exploring and rolling around on the forbidden bed, of course. You probably guessed that outcome before you read the answer. If this is something so predictable and universal that it not only applies to humans but dogs also, then why do we persist to raise people against their nature? Of course, we need boundaries, but for the sake of safety. However, putting up laws and walls around a person shunts their growth like a potted plant and will only make them want to break free. Plant yours in open ground and just trim the branches. Putting up walls also keeps other good people out. One of the most important guidelines we need to realize is that we need both variety *and* moderation. The person who lives his entire life within walls is an oppressed person and has not had one of the greatest and fulfilling joys in life- self-exploration.

As soon as the slightest bit of intelligence is manifested, even in a dog, the life inside will want to explore for itself. The more oppressed a living being is, the more violent their exploration will often tend to be. I snapped like a rubber band desperately trying to find where my natural place was in the world, and I did not go moderately. Like a snapped rubber band my potential burst out of the gate and I fell to the ground. The only information I left home with was that my place was not where my blood family thought it was.

I have tried and will continue to try everything I can in this short life and will write about it. Hopefully a few other things try to kill me and I can write about them too. When you are down the journey up is more impressive. I have tried a very strict Christian religion and my issue is with anything isolationist, I do not have all the answers, but I have that one for sure. My parent's religion is not dissimilar to the Amish that lived amongst us, and for that matter all versions of Christianity are not dissimilar to the Jehovah's Witnesses. Being a Witness and trying to convert Amish is like peeking in a tent and asking them to join you in yours because rain is coming, while both tents are set up in the middle of sunny Times Square. We now live in a connected world, like it or not, it is for the better. I don't want to hear from the person born and raised to be devout in the same religion all his or her life; that is a horse wearing blinders down a narrow road and trotting in the road apples left from the horses before him.

WORLDLY

A devout Jehovah's Witness is no different than a devout Mormon, Muslim, Catholic or Jew. They all feel the same way but hold a different book. I want to hear from the person who has tried all five. I am not a smart man, but I am an experienced man. I earn my intelligence one day at a time.

If someone is different, approach their difference with a question rather than a statement of why you think they are wrong. You cannot say something is wrong that you have not tried and applied. Try their logic. Any matter you try to prove to another person should come from a place of genuine love, not some droning regurgitation of 1 Corinthians 13:4-8.

To love someone is to understand them, not just press your will on them. If you love your teen children, you will try to understand them by asking questions. The more answers you receive the better you may tailor your advice to them. Love is built between individuals, not groups. Never abandon someone if they do not immediately take your advice and never force a square peg into a round hole.

As for your children, they are not a mini-you, that is simple narcissism. They are mini individuals who look like you. Just like they say- there is no instruction manual for rearing children. Why so many parents chose a two-thousand-year-old manual is beyond me, but it didn't work for us. Do not shelter a child from the world, walk them into it and pick them up if they fall until they can safely ride away. What perks my curiosity now is how people will still choose to turn a blind eye to reason and opt instead for safety in the *numbers* of religion. The set of rules my parents chose to follow did not serve them well and to this day they still believe they have it right, above the roughly 40,000 other denominations in the world.

Human beings love to argue and let the point sail right past them. The point of my parent's religion is to preach love, God's love, and to emulate it. They have a code in their faith that they follow which leads them down a path they believe to be righteous, so at least they are striving for nobility. Some people need religion to enlighten their deeper goals, others use it as a weapon. My parents view my free-thinking as a danger so they choose to avoid me, but that is their right. I tend to feel their closed-thinking is a danger to everyone present and future.

The religion I was raised in, the Jehovah's Witnesses, teaches equality among race. This is something that over time has been fighting for its place in common sense, but has become a cornerstone for them. Much effort goes to ensuring that every race feels welcome across that religion. This almost gives the followers a false pride that what they are doing is modern and correct. Race is the *only* recognized equality within this religion. I started to recognize at a young age the hypocrisy I was being taught. Women such as my mother are nowhere near equal to men in this religion even today. They do not hold positions of power and the religion clings to ancient ways of thinking, that womankind is a compliment to mankind. Homosexuals are looked upon as sinful and are not accepted for who they are or offered a home in the congregation. The entire world outside of their religion, so comically named "The Truth" is not looked at as equals.

These great gaping holes in their architecture were my first clue at a young age that what I was involved in was fundamentally wrong. After all, they raised me to have this conscience, but it turned on them. So, I left and my life has been one small social experiment, trying to find the right and wrong fit for our day. This religion has left me out in the rain, but I built my own roof.

Townsend

Religious people such as my parents who predict others will fail if they leave their religion are like people who bet on a rigged game. People like my parents bet on the Yankees (Jehovah's Witnesses) to win the game. They say the Mets (disfellowshipped Jehovah's Witnesses) will undoubtedly fail. The problem with the bet they place is that in this game the Mets were never taught the rules of the game, the Mets suck. They may have been able to watch from the dugout, so when it is their turn at bat they can try to emulate, but they lack any substantial skill.

To really succeed in life, you need to be properly coached. Just like the game of baseball, it takes years of training and practice to succeed in life. Religions like the Jehovah's Witnesses' teach you rules to an entirely different game that rarely apply to actual everyday life in society. Of course, you will have a hard time if you try to leave, you may even fail as I did for a long time. It is completely hypocritical for people of that religion to then look on that failure as their inspiration, or confirmation that their doctrine is somehow correct. They set you up to fail in the first place by secluding you in that doctrine and not allowing you to breathe or see anything else.

WORLDLY

This is the same reason Amish youth often fail during their Rumspringa to connect with the outside world, the religion has bred them to from birth. Rumspringa: a chance the Amish give their kids that even Jehovah's Witnesses do not, a chance to sample the outside world without repercussion. Isolationism is nothing but a doctrine of ignorance and it is nothing short of an abusive way to raise children. Children need discipline based on the real world.

What isolationists take from you is your confidence. They live in fear of a falling sky and pass that down to their children. Meanwhile they are the *same* people *causing* the sky to fall. We are only starting to recognize environmental consequences of our modern civilization. We are now seeing that we have taken our home for granted while we looked to the next one in the sky. The sky really will fall if we do not correct our path, and that would be nothing but self-fulfilled prophesy. You are what you think you are. I may have failed time after time because that is what was expected of me and I believed it. They want you to believe that you cannot survive without their protection from the big scary world. A former member of the Jehovah's Witness cult is left with a self-doubt that is very hard to shake. For eighteen years I have questioned every move I have made, often to the point of paralyzing fear.

Townsend

I have failed so many times that I am comfortable at the bottom- that is where I get my best sleep. I have slept on couches so long that even though I now have a house and a bed, I still prefer the couch. Maybe in some dark corner of my mind lies the comfort that if I fail then at least my parents were not lying to me. Three years ago, I stopped worrying about it, and started believing in myself as a rational human being. Three years ago, my life started to drastically improve.

It took me a long time to realize it, but I do have a purpose. I have experienced things that are best read about from the safety of a couch. I have put myself through a hell that I hope others can learn from and avoid.

I want to be an adult that teaches truth, *real,* actual, truth, proven by scientific method and first-hand experience. My test is a social one and I have learned significantly about society. It has taken more than a decade to see any results and I have lived at rock bottom in the meantime. I hope one day my children can realize that their father went out to test the rain for them. That he did not accept the limited way he was raised and wanted to know the way of the world so he could properly pass it down. There is a danger that human curiosity can also be a drug. I feel empty without the pursuit of knowledge. I see a terribly broken world and I desperately want it fixed. All the wonderful people I have met, that have picked me up when I repeatedly fell, taught me to love and forgive because it is what humans do and not just what a two-thousand-year-old book says to do. Those are the people that make me believe we can still evolve. They are also all people I would not be permitted to know if I was a JW. I have lost a blood family, but I have gained an enormous adopted family with multiple mothers and fathers. I am now an older brother who can tell a younger person the consequences of a decision in detail from memory- not from faith. That is worth more than any amount of money. A story about someone who did one thing in their life and always did it right makes for a boring story.

I never want to give up on a question and admit defeat, which is a difficult task for a curious person. The fact remains however- I do not have all the answers. As a human being I am not rigid, I am dynamic, and I adapt to the evidence I learn. My curiosity gives me constant forward motion, it also helped me stop seeking a party life that after a while becomes just too monotonous with little to learn. That is not to say I do not have a social life. I have a very healthy social life, but I keep it to the weekends and do not drink and drive.

Townsend

It's about moderation. I feel no need to drink habitually because I feel fulfilled and busy with things to do and learn. My curiosity has led me to the next step, to bigger things. My curiosity has been with me forever and is my heavy-handed parent, always offering a life lesson. I do not want to admit "I don't know" and this keeps me learning.

There is one area in particular none of us like to admit we do not know: "Why are we here?" I am not as interested in the *why,* because as the *how* continues to form the "why" becomes less important. Maybe there is no "why". The universe is expanding (and accelerating), but what keeps the human race expanding? I think it is simply the need to know things and grow. We evolve towards what we deem important, and especially now, we need to remember that. The most needed traits are what direct evolution. Perhaps we need to make LCD screens and front door delivery services a little less important before devolution comes knocking (if it hasn't already).

I can't say I believe in an all-knowing God that lives in Heaven and will punish me if I do wrong. To be atheist, or accept the idea we are only organic creatures, tends to lead people immediately to a frightening thought- What horrible people would we turn into without God? The same people we are now of course, it's up to you. It is my belief that we created God, therefore the moral code and its inherent need exists within ourselves. Atheism is not synonymous with evil and immorality. On the contrary, it is my belief that the atheist should be capable of evolving morality to new heights, to continue strengthening the tradition of human ethics beyond the borders of religion. The atheist should be the ethical Jedi, not bound by rigid tradition and rules, however educated by them. The atheist should be held to very high standards because it is the human race he represents, not God.

Atheists should represent everything that is good about mankind. They are not off the hook without a god watching, they are infinitely more so on the hook to prove their point that mankind is good by nature, deserves its place on the top of Earth's food chain and that we can still adapt and/or evolve. I've learned from the past that if I do wrong I will hurt myself. If I do too many drugs I will overdose. If I drink and drive, I will crash and find myself in expensive legal troubles. If I surround myself with the wrong crowd, I will go down with them. Really that message seems to be the point of these 'holy' books anyway, and it really should be common sense. It is those very religions that keep it from becoming common sense but make it into a divine, and profitably tax-free message instead. I have had to learn to adapt and evolve in my own life for survival.

Young or old, life has lasting consequences. They say curiosity killed the cat, but this cat has nine fucking lives. I will not apologize for my curiosity… my curiosity is the best thing I have going. It has led to a full life. My rubber band effect has made me tired at a young age which is why life should be experienced in moderation. If I died tomorrow, at thirty-four years old, I will feel I have had a full life- I have learned and loved- but more importantly… I wrote it down.

Every folly I ever made was a precious lesson. You have to destroy the oyster to get the pearl. I did not need a fear of an angry god to do it. Some people may, and that's just fine. Whatever floats your boat- as long as you are not hurting someone else in the process. Unfortunately, it is extremely rare that by following a strict religion you are not leaving someone else in your wake. My parents (in particular my father) have an attachment, a reliance on religion that outweighed their natural instincts to parent. They were raised in a time of undeveloped psychological diagnoses and I believe there are underlying issues that will probably always remain undiagnosed that helped to feed our families failures. This left us children floating in the wake. In the future I would hope the field does some significant research in the area of a developing concept called "schizotypy", a condition that (among other things) allows people to obsess and take certain religious and social practices way too far.

The way I see it is that every society, at one point in time or another, decided there was a deep need for the conscious mind to recognize its boundaries, for the sake of survival, to raise our children and ensure a safe future for them. Humans have the intellectual capacity to create such a moral code. When we slap a name on it and define every slightly different brand of moral code, human beings will kill each other over the brand name. My own parents have rejected me over their brand name. We have a way of letting the brand name ruin the content.

My current belief is that religion is an overreaction to the idea of God. We made God to better enforce our need for morality. Religion is the result of a human tendency to rip things apart to see how they work, but since it did not really exist in the first place, we got so many differing variations to fight over. The more variations of religion there are the more we should see this true. Religion is not here to stay, not if we continue to evolve and become more intelligent beings. Eventually the masses will understand why we created God to enforce our morals and just take the fruit (the morals) and throw away the useless package. Perhaps too we may learn the impact of what false information can do to thousands of years of human existence and tread more lightly in remembrance of those who died on its account.

The big answers in life are very slippery and they damn sure are not universal. Everyone's journey is different, and that difference is what makes human life so special. The goal of these religions is to stifle individualism and create one big agreeable consciousness. I would like to think we are not like the stuffed aliens in the toy machine in *Toy Story*. There is no way to get every human being to agree on everything under the sun, there are too many off us. The Bible Students started by expressing their individualism and later, as Jehovah's Witnesses have become the polar opposite, creating rules for everything under the sun (such as outlawing masturbation and what you think about every moment of your life) and calling for the end of the world.

WORLDLY

If God is infinite, then he understands the very complexity he created and would not stifle it with cookie-cutter rules designed to make everyone a cog in a giant human-run machine. If you are Christian for example, then God made one thing for you- the Bible. He did not make the religion you joined- a man made that. I have read the Bible six times, cover-to-cover and in my journey through the book I have discerned through its words that religion itself is sinful. Unfortunately, the Bible is almost infinitely malleable, as is evident by the ridiculous number of different interpretations or religions that claim it. One day, maybe mankind still needs another few hundred years (we are not as smart as we like to think), we will realize and define the dangers in the monsters we have born.

So, what's the magic universal advice to help change your life? Like any advice it is broad, and may sound that way also, but you need to truly think about it and mold this to your individual life. I cannot preface this any more than that. There are two words that govern the ability to enjoy a successful, fulfilled, and educated life: variety and moderation. These are two opposing concepts that must work together to have a fulfilling life. Variety is needed to understand the complexity of life, your own self, and to properly educate yourself for a

Townsend

lifetime as a citizen of your generation. Moderation is nothing new and a concept that every religion preaches at its core, but for good reason. A problem exists, in my travels I have never found a religion that preaches the equal importance of both. Variety is absolutely necessary for the same reason that a university education teaches a spectrum of classes to achieve a degree in a single major. Variety is the key to a healthy diet and variety is essential to an effective workout at the gym. Variety is the necessary spice of life, the more you learn that the more you will learn about yourself and your place in the world around you. The more you look outside your hometown the more you will build love for the people outside of it. The more you see the good in things the more you will understand the structure mankind has tried to build to protect it (often unsuccessfully) and why we need structure. We breathe structure, government and religion are broad examples, but our structures should not stifle change.

Moderation will keep you from derailing on your journey for variety. There is a wealth of information out there and to concentrate on one aspect is to deprive yourself of the big picture, but to take it all in at once is impossible and unfocused. We can only take a certain amount of input in a limited amount of time. Just as a body needs a balanced diet, the brain needs a balanced education and a healthy life needs balanced experience. Variety + Moderation = Balance. Do not obsess over money, and do not be a bum. Some of the happiest people I have ever met lived very modestly, but they also paid their bills. The universe is carefully balanced and as part of it we naturally strive to achieve similar balance. I often tried to find stability while teetering in an unbalanced life. Generation to generation we learn, our need for boundaries being one of the first lessons realized. But, to rely on any structure built thousands of years ago for the sake of moderation by people who had access to a fraction of the information we have now is simply inapplicable, although the principles may still apply.

My life has been what many would consider to be a jumbled failure of a mess. I have lacked moderation- but I did learn its importance, and in time, how to apply it. I was raised in a household that only applied one aspect of the two, the typical religious interpretation of moderation, but we definitely lacked the variety my natural curiosity craved. Above all I can say that I am OK. My family has been replaced by Worldly family who took over and loved me where my god-fearing parents failed, and there are many people I consider family.

Townsend

My core, as if it were something in my DNA, drove me to find variety, and if only recently, I have learned moderation. For that reason, I am successful. I have earned a doctorate on human nature. I am glad for every one of my failures; I have come full circle and can understand why I lost my family, from the outside looking in. I am now one of the people my parents would been scared for me to associate with, I know too much. How you raise a child will echo throughout its life. It is my goal that someone may see what I see through reading this and change the way they view their child's mind so that they raise an intelligent, progressive family instead of one like mine that fell victim to systematic ignorance and intolerance. You may have noticed the spacing of this book to be that of a simple, easy read… that's because I also hope a young adult may read my journey and find it helpful to them as well. I hope this to apply to both the teenager and the parent raising them.

If you are currently feeling trapped in the Jehovah's Witness religion, or one of the hundreds of others like it, then you may be scared to leave. I would recommend that you find friends outside of your faith and build a support network. You will need friends as you have most likely lost your family in the process of leaving the pack. Do the opposite of what they demand and make friends with the world, there is a reason they scare you from doing it and it is not because it will kill you.

There are lots of good people out there but be a little skeptical as there are also plenty of bad ones. Look for variety but remember moderation. Find your balance. Keep strong friends who ask little of you except for your company. Keep friends who make you a better person. You need to talk out your issues as well as learn how the world really works. It may be comforting to search for friends going through the same experience, but it is also dangerous to *only* make friends with that type of person as they are deficient in the same areas you are. Have a variety of friends who can coach you through different areas and you will one day be a well-rounded individual who can return the favor. Do not seek out a partner to make you feel more whole. Make yourself whole and look for a partner afterwards. Do not ignore red flags in relationships and do not waste time and energy for self-improvement on improving a terrible relationship. Those good friends you made will help you know if you are in one. Do not expect more answers than questions in your travels, sometimes having the right questions can be satisfying in itself.

Do not be afraid to help yourself, work hard and do not be a mooch. Being a leech will sour your new friends. You need to give as much as you take, but everyone loves a good friend. Be a giver but do not be a pushover. You are in charge... and you are equally responsible for yourself and your actions. Look at the future as an infinite well of learning and drink up. Moderation. Variety.

EPILOGUE

Atheism and evolution are often polarizing beliefs. It is what I believe, I believe it strongly at this point in my life through my own open-minded research and debate, but this book is not a recruitment to join my line of thinking. It is however intended to support everyone's right to pursue life and education *without* losing their family. I hope that someone may make a different decision after reading this book, whether it be to treat their children differently, to escape a faulty belief system, to decide against returning to a religion because someone else wants them to, or to approach their exodus with a level head and avoid trouble. My aim is to promote rational thinking and to bring people together by staying curious and keeping open to *other* people's views on life's journey, not just building walls to keep out the unknown. What is unknown to you is an opportunity for personal growth, not damnation. Every single person has the right to decide for themselves how they see and make sense of our world, while *no one* has the right to impose their understanding on another. Open-minded

Townsend

debate is the forging of intelligent decisions and *that* will be our salvation.

I have seen my parents once during my ten-year high school reunion. At this point in time I have been gone for seventeen years, only seeing my parents that once, and only spoken to them a handful of times via text message or phone call, years pass in between. If we do manage to speak, the topic of their interest is if I have been to a meeting, never what I am doing with my life. I have a brother I barely know; in fact, I know more about the clerk at the local convenience store. Religion is what brought us to this point. I have now lived longer without parents then I did with them. Although the notion of having them back in my life is tempting, I have reasoned that at this point if it ever did happen I doubt we would have enough in common for it to be healthy or rewarding for anyone involved. As for my family, blood is simply not enough. For me to try to change their beliefs now would be like kicking the crutches out from under a crippled person. They would have to realize their whole lives as wasted, riddled with missed opportunities, it is not something I wish for them. I hope they never read this book and continue to finish out their lives in the work they've sacrificed everything for. This book is not for them, it is for others *before* they make the mistakes we have, and for myself. Family is one of life's natural gifts, it may not be until they are gone that you realize what you are missing, please do not do the same.

The Watchtower Bible and Tract Society has since sold off most of Brooklyn Bethel. By 2017, the society had sold 24 properties in Brooklyn that made up the original iconic factory where I had once dreamed to serve. Those properties sold for a current total of almost two-*billion* dollars. $1,949,375,000 to be exact. Most of the factory has been moved upstate to Wallkill, New York, on a 100-hectare property that is more affordable to operate. The society now owns 98 Bethel branches all over the world including, Britain, Germany, and Australia that all report to the New York queen bee. As of 2017 the Watchtower Society still retains 34 properties in Brooklyn, New York, although most are for sale. As of 1990, the Witnesses had 35,811,000 different pieces of literature worldwide. As of 2013 it printed more than a billion Watchtower and Awake magazines each year to be used in preaching and study. The vast staff responsible for printing this literature is comprised solely of volunteers. The organization is funded primarily by donations from field service and more so from its members.

Townsend

I have tried in recent years to make sense of life, and what it means instead of trying to dull its pain. These experiences are not worth regretting; they have become a fuel for thinking and writing. I wrote this primarily for myself, and because well... you have to start somewhere. I wanted to write the entire blur of my twenties to analyze my mistakes.

This book, deeply rooted in truth, is a way for me to understand that those experiences were indeed worth having. Hemmingway said a writer needs to experience life in order to write about it. We have all been through challenging times, my stories are easily topped, I am just the average guy.

Some of the real people represented by characters in this book have been hurt by being near me or by trying to help me. Most of the stories in this book are cringe-worthy and hard to read. Those people are heroes who deserve thanks and I think it is important that those stories are not forgotten but remembered by generations that follow. They carry with them important lessons, lessons that I sincerely hope will call for change. This story exists as a call for change as I don't want anyone else to have those memories except through a gnarly book. The selfless sacrifices people have given me in an attempt to help me all mean something, not just to me but to our society. The cringing nature of this book is by design, and I hope that nature will help the lessons to stick as they did for me. Life is rarely rosy and I, like most, wish I had a time machine to do things differently and never had these experiences to draw on. Books are the closest we get to a time machine.

It is immensely important to scribble on the cave walls, write your experiences and read informative material. In an ironic twist, language is currently under attack by its ally-communication. The dumbing down of communication is evident by the degradation of each language's lexicon. The more you read, the more intelligent you will become, and writing will give your voice immortality. This book as much as anything else, was a self-healing process, however just as I was taught as a child, I am also trying to save others. Try writing for yourself, I sincerely recommend it.

You only live once.

Townsend

Works Cited:

All technical info on Jehovah's Witness organization
(that was not recalled through personal experience) obtained
in the year 2018 though:

https://en.wikipedia.org/wiki/Jehovah%27s_Witnesses

Made in the USA
Las Vegas, NV
10 April 2022